Contents at a Glan

Table of Contents

Introduction

Whether you're a high school students looking for part-time work, a college student looking for your first internship, or a recent grad out in the world looking for your first full-time job, you're taking an important step forward in your life!

Getting a job is not rocket science, but it's also not something to be taken lightly. Part of the process involves figuring out what you want to do and what job will make you happy. The next part is actually identifying the right jobs that are available and applying to them. You also need to prepare your résumé and think about what you want to show employers. After you apply, you want to make sure your application is accepted and that you pass your interviews. And when you get an offer, you need to determine if it's a good package for you.

Finding a job may seem complicated, but my goal in this book is to outline all the steps involved, and help you get through them easily and successfully. Even if you read only part of this book and follow only some of the steps, you'll be better off than most job seekers.

Millions of people have gotten jobs before you. Some have prepared for the task and others haven't. Eventually, people tend to find their way and get on a career path that allows them to succeed. Most likely, you'll change jobs a few times throughout your career and you may also figure out you need to go on a different career path altogether.

Your first job is the beginning of a journey. With this book, you get a good start and you'll be armed with the knowledge, tools, and best practices that will help you as you progress along your career path.

About This Book

Finding your first job may seem like a daunting task, but with this book, it won't be. Here I provide a comprehensive overview of the various steps involved in finding out what job you'll like, going after that job, and getting the job. This book provides practical tips you can use and doesn't go into philosophical discussions or technical jargon. The knowledge in this book is a combination of common sense and advice that has helped job seekers over the years.

Each part of the book addresses a facet of the search, and each chapter and section addresses a specific step you can take to make your search a lot easier. You can jump from one section of the book to another, in any order, depending on where you are in your search.

Within this book, you may note that some web addresses break across two lines of text. If you're reading this book in print and want to visit one of these web pages, simply key in the web address exactly as it's noted in the text, pretending as though the line break doesn't exist. If you're reading this as an e-book, you've got it easy — just click the web address to be taken directly to the web page.

Foolish Assumptions

Everyone's circumstances are unique; however, I've seen some patterns over the years on how people look for work and where they need help. I made the following assumptions about you as I wrote this book:

>> **You have some college experience.** A few chapters, not all, make reference to college activities, internships, and resources. This applies if you went to vocational school, community college, a four-year university, or graduate school. Even if you didn't go to college, the content in this book is pertinent and will help you get your first job.

>> **You're tight on time.** Looking for your first job is hard enough, and you shouldn't have to read a novel to figure out how to do it right. This book gives you advice in small digestible pieces that you can easily access.

>> **You have a computer and Internet access.** Most of the steps outlined in this book rely on your leveraging online tools to achieve what you need to do. Whether it's searching for jobs, researching employers, or doing an online assessment, you need fast Internet access. You can do a lot of the things outlined here on your phone, but it's better if you sit down in front of your computer, calmly and with a big enough screen, to do things such as write a cover letter and submit your job applications. Go to your public library to use a computer if you don't have one at home.

>> **You're on social media.** It's rare to find individuals who are not on social media, and only a few stay away from it. Your social media presence impacts how employers perceive you and helps you connect with others. Some of the chapters in this book reference sites like Facebook and Twitter, and I assume you have an account on at least one of these.

Icons Used in This Book

I use the following icons throughout this book to highlight important information that allows you to make the most out of the advice provided:

The Tip icon points out pertinent insights and shortcuts to other parts of the book that make getting your first job even easier.

I use the Remember icon to flag information that's so useful you'll want to commit it to memory.

I use the Warning icon to draw your attention to things that could save you a lot of time and trouble.

When I share information that's interesting but not essential to your understanding of the subject at hand, I mark it with the Technical Stuff icon. You can skip anything marked with this icon without missing the main point.

Beyond the Book

In addition to the content in this book, you also get access to a free online Cheat Sheet filled with more pointers on how to get your first job. The Cheat Sheet includes advice such as how to evaluate your first job offer and how to keep track of your applications. To access this resource go to www.dummies.com and enter **Getting Your First Job For Dummies Cheat Sheet** in the search box.

Where to Go from Here

Depending on where you are in the job search process, you can use the Table of Contents and Index to easily locate the section that will solve your need.

You don't have to read this book in order from beginning to end — you can jump to any section that interests you! If you're not sure where to begin, I recommend you start with Chapter 1 to help you get organized prior to starting your search. If you're not sure what you want to do or what kind of job you want, Chapter 3 is a huge help. And because this book is about getting your first job, you should also make sure to read Chapter 6, which goes into the technical details of how to do an effective job search.

Finally, no matter where you are in your job search, check out Chapters 10 and 11 to get tips on how to do well in your interviews. Most job seekers consider interviewing to be one of the hardest parts of the process. Read these chapters to gain confidence!

I was in your shoes once, trying to figure out what I wanted to do and how to get started. But you're farther ahead because you're reading this book! You've got this. Now, onward and upward!

1

Preparing Yourself Before the Job Search

Set objectives and use the right tools as you embark on finding your first job.

Take an inventory of your skills and abilities so you can highlight them on your résumé and in your interactions with employers.

Learn more about yourself and get a better idea of what you might like to do by using online assessment tools.

Discover different career paths by talking to others about their work and researching occupations.

Chapter **1**

Mapping Out Your Job Search Strategy

What kind of job are you looking for and what do you want to get out of it?

Your answers to these questions determine how long it will take you to find your first job. They also establish what you'll need to do to get the job. For example, if your goal is to get part-time work, of any kind so you can earn some money, then you don't need to do a lot of research. For the most part, it's about going to places like Starbucks and Applebee's to fill out applications. It may take you a few days or a few weeks to get a part-time job.

On the other hand, if you have a plan in mind, where you want a highly coveted job after college and you know you'll have competition, then you have to start thinking about the internships you need to have in order to improve your chances of getting that job. It may take you up to three months, and sometimes even a year and a half to land the job you like, depending on whether you have relevant experience.

Even entry-level jobs sometimes require experience. This is a Catch-22. You're looking for your first job, but you need previous experience. Internships are a perfect way to gain this experience!

This chapter talks about the various types of first jobs you can have. You also get an overview of tools to use to stay organized.

Getting Your First Part-Time Job

Your first job will most likely be a part-time one, as is the case for the majority of us. My first job was as an office assistant for the library director's office at Stanford University. I got this job my freshman year. It paid well and it was on campus, close to my dorm and on my way to classes.

The work involved delivering interoffice mail and submitting expense reports to the travel office. I also made photocopies and did office-related work that needed to be done.

Part-time jobs abound. They can be in an office setting, in a retail location such as Walmart or Macy's, or in the food service industry at locations such as Starbucks, In-N-Out, Panda Express, and other similar businesses.

Although not glamorous, part-time work provides you with at least these three benefits:

>> **Money:** This is the obvious benefit. Unless you're volunteering for a nonprofit, you need to get paid for your time and effort. A part-time job gives you spending money.

>> **Flexibility:** This is one of the key benefits, especially if you're in school or have other obligations. While you're in school, your focus should be on your education and not so much on work. A part-time job gives you the flexibility to earn money on a schedule that fits around your classes.

>> **Work ethic:** This is often an understated benefit, but your first job is also the way you learn about the value of working hard and working with others. A job also forces you to be on time and teaches you to deliver on your commitments. Future employers will infer you have these qualities when they see your work experience.

REMEMBER

An employer looking at two almost-identical résumés will most likely pick the one with the previous work experience, regardless of the work, compared to the one that doesn't have any work experience.

Getting part-time work is usually easier than getting an internship or a full-time job. You can either walk in and apply in person or go online and submit an application. It may take you a few days or two to four weeks to find a part-time job if you focus on it. And the less picky you are about the job, the more likely you are to find one sooner.

Some employers will require a résumé while others won't. Either way, make sure to have your résumé handy in case the employer asks for a copy.

TIP

Check out Chapter 8 for help with crafting a great résumé.

Securing Internships

Having at least one internship under your belt will greatly improve your chances of getting a good job when you graduate from college. According to AfterCollege, doing at least one internship while in college means you're six times more likely to have a job lined up by graduation compared to those who didn't have any internships.

Internships add experience to your résumé and they help you get in the door, especially at highly coveted employers. Here are some of the things you get with the right internship:

>> **Gain experience.** They give you relevant knowledge in a field or industry. This helps convince employers down the line that you have relevant knowledge, improving your chances of getting a great first job.

>> **Try before you buy.** Hopefully you have great internships and value the experience you gain. But if you don't have a good experience, this is still okay. An internship lets you figure out what an employer is like or what an entire industry is about. It gives you a reality check so you can make sure you want to pursue the path you've put yourself on. If you like the employer and the industry, you can keep moving forward with confidence. If not, then you have time to consider a different path and different employers before you graduate.

>> **Get your foot in the door.** Some employers also like to try before they buy. They invest time and resources into creating internship programs that serve as pipelines to hire new college graduates. Often, an internship can serve as your ticket to a full-time job after you graduate. So, if you have a company you really want to work for, focus on getting an internship there.

>> **Make contacts.** A good internship allows you to develop professional relationships with fellow interns and with the employer. If you do a good job and like the employer, you may get invited to apply for a full-time job upon graduation. You may also make contacts who can recruit you into other organizations if they decide to move on.

>> **Fill your résumé.** At a minimum, internships provide material to fill your résumé and they show you have experience. The employer name, if it's a recognizable one, also adds value.

REMEMBER

An internship shouldn't be primarily about the money. The experience and insights you gain and the ability to list the experience in your résumé are far more valuable.

An internship doesn't have to be full-time for you to benefit from it. If you need the money and take an unpaid internship or a low-paying one, consider doing it part-time. You can then use any remaining hours in your day to work a part-time job that pays you well.

Internships, especially good ones, are hard to get. Start looking for these early and do the following:

>> **Leverage on-campus resources.** Go to your university career center to see how it can help you secure an internship.

>> **Start looking in the fall.** Most students look for jobs and internships from January to May before they graduate. Start earlier to get ahead of the pack.

>> **Use your connections.** Ask friends and family connections for help. An internship lasts a few months only. Ask your parents, aunts, and uncles if they can call in favors and help get you an internship.

TIP

Read Chapter 5 to learn about the resources you can use to find an internship.

Finding Your First Job after College

Your first job marks a major milestone in life as it sets the course of your career path. So, in other words, make sure you find a job you like. You should plan on staying at your job for at least 18 months in order to make a meaningful contribution. That's also enough time for you to start building a professional network, and to make a good impression.

The more time and attention you put into your search, the more likely you are to get the job you want. It can take months to find the right job, especially if you wait until the end of your college years.

Here are some ways to ensure you speed up your search:

>> **Sign up for on-campus interviews.** Most colleges have employers who come to interview on campus. The process is similar to a conveyor belt, with events such as information sessions and deadlines of when to sign up for interview slots. Make sure you sign up to interview with some of these employers. Being on the conveyor belt ensures you get exposed to opportunities. Missing it could lower your chances of having a job when you graduate.

>> **Have internships.** Previous internship experience matters. It gives you a leg up by giving you exposure to previous employers who may also offer you full-time employment upon graduation. It also makes you stand out above those who haven't had internships.

>> **Start early.** Start looking for your first job early in the academic year or even a year before you graduate. Yes, this is easier said than done. You don't have to go full on and look for a job. You can start exploring at your own pace.

Knowing the Importance of Your First Job

Your first job, whether it's an internship or a full-time one, is important for many reasons. It determines your career trajectory. It can set you up for success if everything aligns or it can give you a slow start if for some reason it doesn't work out as expected. Knowing the different aspects to consider in your first job allows you to make a better decision on which opportunities to pursue.

Getting exposed to an industry

More important than the employer is the industry in which you're getting into. If you go to work for an insurance company, you'll gain knowledge and eventually some expertise in the insurance field. Likewise, if you go work at a company like Facebook, you'll be in tech, and more specifically, in the media space.

Whatever job you choose, make sure you have some interest in the industry to which the employer belongs, and think about where you'd like to spend some meaningful amount of time in the space.

Are you going into an industry that's growing or one that is in a state of change? You may thrive in one that is looking to innovate, such as the media space where news is evolving from print to digital. Or you may choose to play it safe and go into a proven space like tech.

Doing the job itself

The actual work you'll be doing will move you to specialize in a certain area and you'll gain a specific set of skills. Having an idea of what kind of work you'll do in a job will give you insight into what types of skills you'll acquire over time. Make sure these are the skills you want to develop.

For example, if you choose to take a sales role, you'll learn about sales techniques and develop certain skills sets. Over time, you'll know if this is the job for you. Will you like constantly interacting with people or would you rather have a role behind the scenes?

Building your professional network

Your first job is not just about what you do but also about whom you do it with. Having good colleagues with whom you can collaborate makes all the difference in the world. These are individuals who will help you in your career. They can pull you with them to other organizations as they move.

You can also hire them to go work with you if you ever decide to go to another employer.

The right group of co-workers can help increase your chances of being successful, both at your current job and throughout your career.

Setting a Goal for Yourself

As I mention earlier, it can take months or even over a year to find your first job, depending on what you're looking for.

Setting goals helps people complete a certain task or challenge faster than they would if they didn't have any milestones at all.

Here are some ways to use goals in order to find your first job faster:

>> **Set an overall goal.** By when do you want to have a job? This could be a month from now or next year. Whatever your date, set a stake in the ground and make a goal for yourself to motivate yourself to start looking.

>> **Create small milestones.** A distant goal always looks achievable, but as it approaches, you may find yourself struggling to meet your own deadline. Create small goals for yourself on when you want to write your résumé and when you want to apply for your first job.

If you miss your own internal deadlines, it's okay. The point is to put a stake in the ground and take steps forward, instead of lingering and never moving.

Having expectations

The time and effort it takes to find your first job is often directly correlated to the quality of the employer. In other words, if you're applying for a job at a well-known employer like Google or Facebook, expect to have a lot of competition and expect the process to take longer. Employers with a well-known consumer brand attract a lot of job seekers. As a result, they can take their time in choosing whom they hire.

On the other hand, if you find a job you like at an employer that is not well known, then you should have less competition and an easier time getting in the door.

This was the case for me when I graduated from college. I wanted to learn more about the web and the Internet, so I applied for a job as a project coordinator at a little-known company called BBN. BBN was started by the people who invented the Internet. The modem was also invented at BBN, and the person who invented email and decided to put the @ sign between the username and the domain name also worked at BBN.

The company didn't have a well-known employer brand, but it was a great company nonetheless. BBN invented so much technology and hired a lot of smart people (I may have been the exception). When BBN recruiters went to interview at Stanford, not many students applied to interview with them because no one knew about BBN. I had waited until the last minute my senior year to apply for jobs (the opposite of what I preach in this book) because I didn't know what I wanted to do. So I applied to BBN, was interviewed, and ended up getting the job. I got lucky.

The moral of this story is to be aware that if you apply to a popular employer, you may have to work harder and wait longer than if you apply to a less popular organization.

My advice to you is to start early and to put in the hard work to get the job you want, regardless of the employer's popularity.

Creating a timeline

To get an idea of how long it may take you to get your first job, create a simple timeline and keep it the back of your mind as a reminder. Table 1-1 illustrates the steps involved in the job search process and gives estimates of how long each step may take.

REMEMBER

The time it takes to get a job depends on whether you're looking for a part-time job, an internship, or a full-time role.

TABLE 1-1   **Figuring Out How Long It Will Take You to Find Your First Job**

Step	Time Expected
Job search	Four to five weeks. More if you don't find anything you like.
Interviews	Two to three weeks. It depends if they happen all at once or if you spread them out over time.
Hear back	One to two weeks to get a response from the recruiter. You may hear back sooner or unfortunately not at all in some cases.
Job offer	One week. When you hear that you're getting an offer, it may take up to a week to get it in writing.
Offer acceptance	Up to one week. When you get a written offer, the employer will ask you to respond as soon as you can. You may be given a few days or a week at most.

Searching for the right first job could take you up to three months. This is just one scenario. In theory, you could also walk into the restaurant around the corner, apply for a job as a server, and get the job on the spot if the employer needs someone badly and you have the relevant experience or a great personality.

On the other hand, if you're still trying to figure out what to do, you could spend months searching without knowing what you're looking for. Some job seekers have spent up to 18 months looking for their first jobs.

TIP

Having a plan and knowing what you want will help speed up your search. Check out Chapter 3.

Organizing Your Search with Online Tools and Apps

Looking for a job is not complicated, it's just tedious. The more jobs you apply to, the better your chances of getting one. But this also means that you have more steps to consider and more deadlines to track. You can take the stress out of the job search and avoid mistakes by using some of these applications.

Using Google Calendar

Google's free calendar is a great simple way to stay organized. If you don't already have a calendar on your phone, use this tool. Google Calendar comes with your Google Gmail account. These accounts are free, and you most likely already have one via your school.

Access the calendar by going to `http://calendar.google.com`.

TIP

Here are some ways to stay organized:

>> **Enter deadlines.** Write down dates when you need to submit applications or sign up for campus interviews. Set yourself at least a day's reminder to that you get a notification with enough notice so you can prepare for the specific deadline. You don't want to miss out on an opportunity because you forgot about the application date.

>> **Set goals.** Are you putting off writing your résumé? Enter a date and time when you want to start working on it. Carve out one to two hours on your calendar and force yourself to start working on your résumé and cover letter.

>> **Create follow-up reminders.** When you apply for jobs or have interviews, set future follow-up reminders for yourself, a week or two ahead of when you want to follow up with a recruiter to ask about the status of your application.

TIP

Save time and lower your stress. Enter interviews dates on your calendar along with the address of where they'll be held and the name of your point of contact. You don't want to be scrambling the day of the interview to figure out where to go.

Taking notes with Evernote

Take notes. Whether it's on a sheet of paper, on a notepad, or on a text file on your laptop, it's important to write down what you learn at information sessions, interviews, and career fairs. I use a tool called Evernote. The basic version is free, but you can pay a premium to get extra storage and to access your notes from more than two devices. I like Evernote because I can write ideas down on my phone and then access them on my laptop and vice versa.

I'm always on my phone, and I tend to have ideas at random points throughout the day. Having a tool where I can write things down quickly and reference them later is very helpful.

Download Evernote by going to `www.evernote.com`.

Using Google Sheets

Spreadsheets are great to make lists of items you want to compare — for example, job offers! I prefer Google Sheets because you can save your work online and access it from anywhere.

Here are some examples of how you can use Google Sheets:

» Write a list of jobs to which you want to apply with notes and deadlines next to each one.

» Create a spreadsheet of job offers along with the components of the offer next to each so you can more easily compare and contrast them.

» Make a sheet of the cities you would consider moving to along with the cost of rent and food for each, so you can calculate your true cost of living once you get offers.

Use Google Sheets by going to http://sheets.google.com.

TIP

Visit the Cheat Sheet to get ideas of how to create a comparison of job offers and how to track your applications.

Expanding your vocabulary with Thesaurus.com

This is a great site to use when writing thank-you notes and when working on your résumé. You don't want to repeat the same verb over and over. Use Thesaurus.com to find different ways to say things and to improve your résumé and cover letter.

Avoid repeating the same word and find synonyms by going to www.thesaurus.com.

Chapter 2

Highlighting What You Bring to an Employer

Searching for your first job is about looking inward as much as it is about looking outward.

During the course of your job search, you'll need to talk about yourself, including your strengths and your accomplishments. You'll need to include these attributes in your résumé and cover letter. They'll also come up during your interviews.

In this chapter, you get guidance on how to identify your skills and abilities based on your previous school projects, activities, and field of study.

Your friends and family often know you better than you know yourself. Here you cover how to approach those close to you so they can help you to better talk about yourself. This allows you to be more prepared for interviews and it also lets you create a résumé faster.

Identifying Your Skills

Employers will ask you about your skills and how they pertain to the job to which you're applying. Knowing your skills helps you prepare your responses and it also allows you to better identify jobs where you can do well, based on those skills.

There are two kinds of skills:

>> **Hard skills:** These are ones you learn, like programming, doing financial accounting, or sorting mail accurately and quickly. Playing guitar is another example of a hard skill. These are concrete, tangible skills that help you perform specific tasks.

>> **Soft skills:** These are a mix of your personality traits and natural abilities. An example of a soft skill is being a good listener. Another one is being tenacious, meaning that you don't give up. The first skill is valuable in many settings, including healthcare where you need to listen to patients. The second one can apply to sales or any other role that is goal driven.

You could argue that soft skills can be learned as well, but these tend to be baked into your personality. In this section, I explain how you can uncover these skills.

Translating your major into specific skills

Your major in college translates into a number of skills that you can list on your résumé and talk to employers about. For example, if your major is computer science, then programming is one of your skills. Creating algorithms is another. If you're majoring in economics, then critical thinking is another skill you can point to.

TIP

Your academic department may have a map of your major and related skills. Ask your department administrator if he has this data or look for it on your department's website.

Employers will know your major by looking at your résumé. What you really want them to know is what you can do. This is more obvious for specialized majors such as nursing, computer science, and actuarial science. But the possibilities are wider for majors where it's more about the skills than the specialization. Majors that are not specialized and are more likely to lead you into various jobs include business, English, and psychology. Think about what you do in your classes and create a list of skills associated with those courses.

Table 2-1 shows some examples of skills associated with some popular majors.

TABLE 2-1   ## Popular Majors and Associated Skills

Major	Relevant skills
Accounting	Forecasting, using spreadsheets, financial reporting, financial analysis
Anthropology	Doing research, documenting, interviewing, reporting, statistics
Biology	Doing research, documenting, analyzing data
Business	Reading comprehension, communication, writing, qualitative analysis, analyzing data
Chemistry	Math, reading comprehension, research, analyzing data, device operation
Economics	Critical thinking, communication, math, reading comprehension, problem solving, statistics
Education	Communication, training, organization, leadership, time management
Electrical engineering	Critical thinking, programming, doing math, quantitative analysis, problem solving, statistics
English	Writing, being creative, critical thinking, communication, qualitative analysis
Humanities	Research, writing, communication, critical thinking, qualitative analysis, presenting
Industrial engineering	Math, data analysis, quality control, statistics, optimization
Marketing	Presenting, market research, A/B testing, telling stories
Mathematics	Math, focus, logical thinking, problem solving
Nursing	Active listening, patience, responsiveness, clinical knowledge, device operation
Philosophy	Critical thinking, constructing arguments, creativity
Psychology	Reading comprehension, active listening, communication, doing research
Physics	Doing research, math, device operation, quantitative analysis, qualitative analysis, problem solving

REMEMBER

This is just a sample list of the skills associated with each major. The same skills can also apply to more than one major.

Some skills such as being good at math are highly transferable. For example, if you're a math major, it shows you're good at problem solving and means you can most likely learn how to program fairly easily. If you study nursing, it shows you're good with patients. You could also go into the pharmaceutical industry and work on clinical trials with patients who are testing new drugs. A degree in education can help you become a teacher, but it also allows you to take on training jobs — for example, training a sales team on how to use a company's new products. You get the idea.

TIP

Majors have skills associated with them that are transferable to different types of jobs. Highlight the relevant skills that apply to the job you're pursuing.

Listing your soft skills

You may have some unique ability or personality trait that doesn't necessarily apply to your major or job but that nonetheless is worth listing. Employers want to see not only what you know but also what you're like as a person. Your personal attributes can help you do certain jobs better. You probably won't list these on your résumé, but they may come up in interviews.

Examples of soft skills include the following:

>> **Calm:** Being able to remain calm in stressful situations is a great quality to have. This is a trait worth mentioning if the job you're considering involves a lot of stress.

>> **Curious:** Being curious means you're willing to learn about new things. Employers value individuals who want to learn and improve their skills.

>> **Dependable:** If others are able to depend on you, this is good for the employer to know. In your job, you'll be expected to deliver on your commitments and complete the work you're given.

>> **Empathetic:** Having empathy and caring about others is a noble thing. This may not be an important trait if you're going to be a financial analyst, but it's definitely a great trait if you'll be dealing with patients or customers.

>> **Independent:** Employers like to see individuals who are self-reliant and don't require a lot of guidance or supervision.

>> **Good listener:** Being a good listener means you can follow direction and absorb information. Listening also helps you in sales roles and in healthcare settings when dealing with patients.

>> **Outgoing:** Having an outgoing personality helps for a variety of roles, ranging from sales to healthcare, marketing to engineering. It implies that you like to communicate, and communication is vital for teamwork.

>> **Tenacious:** If you're tenacious, it means you're driven to complete a task, no matter how difficult and to reach your goals. Employers love this attribute. This should not be confused with being stubborn, which implies that you stick to your opinions, even when reason says otherwise.

TIP

Think about your unique skills and abilities and list the ones that are relevant to the job. Be ready to give the employers examples of how you practice these soft skills.

Uncovering your hidden skills

You may have some abilities or traits that you take for granted, yet to an employer, these traits could be valuable. These traits can include obvious things like the following:

>> **Ability to lift weight:** Maybe you weightlift and can carry up to 200 pounds without a problem. Some jobs, especially warehouse ones, require that you lift heavy packages.

>> **Being a good chess player:** Being a good chess player may just mean you're good at chess. It can also imply that you're good at strategy and knowing how to anticipate a competitor's moves. If you excel at chess, list it on your résumé or bring it up during your interviews.

>> **Good memory:** Having a photographic memory, or just a good one, is important for remembering facts and data. Most people talk about employers valuing critical thinking. But memorization is important, too. Being able to remember pieces of information is key for process-oriented jobs.

>> **Laser focus:** Being able to focus your full attention on a task and do it well is an important character trait of a productive employee. Do you live in a noisy household or live with distracting roommates yet are able to do your homework well? If so, then you possess a valuable skill.

Getting feedback from your friends

Your family and good friends are usually the best at judging what you're good at and where you need to improve. These are the people who have spent the most time with you. They may be able to identify your strengths and capabilities better than you can.

Your mom, for example, may be biased and say you're the best in the world to do any job. But still, it's worth asking your parents, siblings, significant other, and friends these questions:

>> What are some of my best qualities? Why?

>> What would you say I'm good at doing? Can you give me some examples?

>> What are some of my flaws or areas where I can improve? Why?

Write all the answers down, even if you get feedback jokingly. There's probably some truth behind it. You may learn something about yourself that you didn't know. This feedback will help you to write your résumé, and it will also aid you tremendously in preparing for interviews, where you'll be asked to identify your strengths and areas for improvement.

TIP

Check out Chapter 11 to get an idea of questions to expect during your interviews.

Identifying areas for improvement

You can normally count on your friends and family to be honest with you. Just as they will tell you about your great qualities, they will also tell you about your flaws.

Make note of the feedback not only to identify areas where you need to improve but also to note which of these areas you'll tell employers about when asked.

Here are some sample traits that you can work on improving, but you should *not* tell employers about:

>> **Bad temper:** Nobody likes people with bad tempers. Work on controlling yours, but don't tell an employer about it unless you're specifically asked.

>> **Lack of patience:** We all lose our patience at some point, especially when overwhelmed. Patience is a virtue, and the lack of it is not well perceived.

>> **Stubbornness:** If you're stubborn like a mule, you should work on being more open. Being stubborn implies that you're set in your ways even when common sense says that you should do otherwise. This is a character trait best not mentioned.

On the other hand, here are some examples of flaws where it's okay to tell the employer as long as you put a positive spin on them:

>> **Not delegating:** This is a strong negative if you're a manager, but if you're just starting out it's fine to tell the employer. Although it is an area to improve, it's also a sign that you're not afraid to take on work and that you do what needs to get done.

>> **Being an introvert:** This is not necessarily a bad trait, especially if you're in an individual contributor role where you don't need to interact a lot with others. You can mention this as an area of improvement. If you have examples of how you've overcome it, even better.

>> **Worrying too much:** Do you tend to stress a lot about certain things? Being able to control stress is a good quality. On the other hand, an employer can interpret your tendency to worry in a positive light because it means you'll worry about doing a good job.

WARNING

Improve where you can and don't feel compelled to share your weak spots with employers. But be ready to talk about them when asked.

Detailing Your Experience

Employers looking for entry-level candidates often want to see some kind of experience on your résumé. If you've had internships or part-time jobs, even in high school, then it's easier to showcase this experience.

But if this is your first job, you need something to show an employer that you have some history where you've performed work or collaborated with others on completing a task or achieving a goal. Ultimately, this is what experience is meant to show.

Your school projects, hobbies, and other activities can serve you well in showing employers that you have relevant experience.

Taking note of volunteer work

Volunteer work counts as experience. The only difference is that you aren't paid for this work — but it's still work. It also shows that you're a caring and involved individual who takes an active role in the community.

Here are some examples of volunteer activities:

>> **Teaching Sunday school:** If you go to church and volunteer at Sunday school, this is a notable activity to highlight. It shows that you can mentor others. It also conveys your commitment to get up every Sunday morning to show up for class while your friends may be sleeping in. And it implies that you have patience, because this is a required trait when working with a group of kids.

>> **Tutoring others:** Do you volunteer to tutor students in math, science, or another subject? This shows you have mastery of a field and are able to share your knowledge with others.

>> **Mentoring kids:** If you're part of an organization like the Boy Scouts or Girl Scouts and mentor younger scouts, list this as relevant experience on your

résumé. These activities are often associated with developing leadership skills. Another good example is volunteering with Boys & Girls Clubs and Big Brothers Big Sisters.

>> **Technical support volunteer:** Do you maintain the website or related technology for a school or nonprofit group? This is also relevant experience you can highlight, no matter how easy the work may seem to you. It shows that you know technology and that you're interested in applying it to good causes.

>> **Fundraising:** Have you ever participated in a fundraising event such as Run for Life or an auction for a school? These activities are worth mentioning, especially if you were involved in raising large amounts of funds or if you helped mobilize people for a cause. If you can fundraise, it means you're organized, you're able to motivate people, and you're driven by goals.

Listing school projects

School projects can also count as relevant experience, especially if you worked with a group or achieved something that was challenging. Here are some examples:

>> **Business case studies:** Marketing and business courses often have a project component where you work on a case study or on a real-world challenge that a local business faces. These projects are usually done with a team, and you present the results of your project at the end of the semester. If you worked on a case study that delivered tangible results and feedback to an organization, or if the case study received high marks, list it as part of your experience. These case studies help showcase your ability to work with a team, to think critically, and to solve problems.

>> **Technical challenges:** Coding projects or technical competitions are great highlights to include on your résumé. For example, participating in online coding challenges where you achieve a certain technical rank is worth nothing. In one extreme, if you're involved in creating a self-driving car or a robot that can achieve a certain task independently, then employers may heavily recruit you.

TIP

Check with your school's career center to see if it offers an e-portfolio tool to help you keep track of your school projects and writing assignments.

Showcasing notable sports and hobbies

Sports and hobbies are also important to show on your résumé and profile. In fact, many employers look to hire athletes for sales-related roles because some of the traits that athletes have are the same ones that make salespeople successful.

Table 2-2 illustrates some of activities that can give employers a hint of your qualities and attributes.

TABLE 2-2

Sample Activities with Related Traits

Activity	Relevant Traits
Sports	Teamwork, competitiveness, drive, commitment, strength
Team captain or manager	Leadership, ambition, strength
Cooking	Attention to detail, creativity, outgoing
Ballroom dancing	Creativity, stamina, outgoing, art appreciation
Track and field	Competitiveness, strength, endurance
Martial arts	Discipline, strength, art and cultural appreciation
Juggling	Coordination, creativity, discipline
Playing a musical instrument	Creativity, mathematically inclined, discipline

TIP

Whatever your hobby or special interest, even if it's participating in hot-dog-eating contests, include it. What you do shows a bit of who you are, and it gives the employer an idea of the qualities you have to do a job well.

Sharing your background

Your unique life circumstances can help you tell your story to an employer. The head of university recruiting for a major global technology company, someone I deeply respect, along with her team, used to tell me that she wouldn't put too much emphasis on a student's GPA when making hiring decisions. This is because not all students are able to focus on academics. Some students are luckier than others and can focus entirely on school without needing to work. Others may be working to support their family while also taking a full course load. This can affect their ability to get the highest GPA.

Not all recruiting teams are as aware and mindful as this group. Which is why it's good to talk about your circumstances if the opportunity arises during conversation. You don't need to make people feel sorry for you or create a sympathy story. And you shouldn't. But it's okay to share any special circumstances as long as the opportunity comes up and you don't have to go out of your way to do this.

On the flip side, it's also good to share circumstances that give you perspective. Examples of life circumstances that may come up in conversation can include the following:

>> **Living in different countries:** If you lived in other countries, this gives you perspective and shows that you're open to other ideas and cultures. This tends to be a quality highly desired by employers. If you speak another language, that's even better. You could be hired to represent or do work for an organization in the specific country.

>> **Constantly moving:** If you constantly moved as a child because of your family's work, whether because a parent was in the military or had a private-sector job, this shows that you're accustomed to change. Organizations, especially large ones, are constantly changing. You can weave your experiences into your cover letter when you talk about why you're a good fit for an organization.

>> **Being in foster care:** Being a foster child could mean that you had to deal with uneasy change as a child. Although it's personal, your story could be an interesting one to share with an employer if appropriate and if it comes up.

TIP

Keeping your personal life separate from work is a good rule of thumb and employers are not supposed to pry into your personal space. But if the opportunity arises to talk about yourself during an interview, it's okay to mention some of your experiences. They shape who you are and help the employers know more about you.

Chapter **3**

Figuring Out What You Want to Do

F inding your first job is an important task in life. Even more important is knowing what you want to do in your career. Most of us struggle to find the job that will truly make us happy. And many people go through life at a job that may earn them good income, but not necessarily give them satisfaction or a sense of accomplishment.

If you've already figured out what path you want to take, then you're farther ahead than most and you should consider yourself lucky. If you've always known you wanted to be a flight attendant, a cardiologist, a dentist, a pharmacist, or a police officer, then you're already on a well-defined path.

On the other hand, if you studied business, marketing, or math, you have a wide array of possibilities you can pursue. Even if you're studying nursing, a very noble and defined profession, you still need to figure out your specialty, whether it's pediatrics, NICU, ER, or another area. The same decisions go with just about any other field or major.

Read this chapter to learn about resources that can help you figure out what to do. You get walk-throughs of services that guide you in your quest to finding your calling. You also get guidance on how to reach out to others, so you can see what they do and figure out if it's what you want to do.

You may decide you want to do something different later in life. But for now, you'll get help on where to start.

Taking Self-Assessments

The first step in figuring out what you want to do is to learn more about yourself. Self-assessment tests and games are a good way to do this. Self-assessments vary in what they do and how they measure, but in general, they let you learn about yourself by collecting information about your work preferences, personality, and other traits. These tests are only as good as the results they show you and depending on what actionable steps you can take with the results you're given.

Getting a test score or a number on an assessment is all fine and good for having a conversation about it at dinner. But what you should really expect from assessments is to get recommendations on what types of jobs and careers you should be focusing on based on the results. These evaluations are not the end-all and be-all in helping you decide what you should do, but they can add to the guidance you receive as you ponder what job to pursue.

TIP

Use assessments to learn about possible careers. But never let these evaluations dissuade you from a possible career or job you may want to pursue.

Playing Mercer Match

Mercer Match, powered by Pymetrics, is an impressive tool that lets you learn more about yourself through games. You can play these games for free on your laptop or on your smartphone through an app you can download. Underlying these games is decades-long neuroscience research that helps you identify top skills and traits as you complete the various games.

To use Mercer Match, just go to www.mercermatch.com, register for an account, and log in and start playing games!

You can go through a series of games that will test for various attributes. In one example, you get to inflate balloons. With each pumping of the balloon, you get some money. But if the balloon pops, you lose the money you've accumulated. One of the attributes tested here is your propensity for risk. Are you willing to risk the balloon popping to try to maximize your gain or will you take the conservative approach and only pump the balloon a few times?

After you've played for a period of time, you'll get a report that shows you your top traits. More important, and more useful, you'll get a list of top career matches, as shown in Figure 3-1. In my case, the top three matches were Sales and Trading, Accounting, and Project Management.

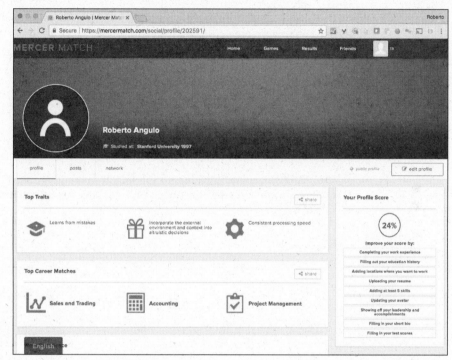

FIGURE 3-1: Seeing your results and top traits on Mercer Match.

Mercer Match got at least two of these right. In my job, I do a lot of selling — selling to new members to join our team and to more employers and universities to use AfterCollege. I also like looking at numbers to make informed decisions. And my first job out of college was as a project manager. I didn't like or dislike project management, but I was good at it.

TIP

Take the top career matches recommended by Mercer Match and plug them in the search box of your favorite job board to see what jobs and internships you find. For a list of sites to use, turn to Chapter 16.

Using Paddle

Paddle is another great tool that helps you figure out what you like and gives you insight into what sectors may be of interest to you. It's also free to take the assessment and to get a basic report. Instead of using games, Paddle takes you through a series of A versus B type questions — about 45 of them — so that it can learn about you.

The science behind Paddle is based on research initiated by Matthew Thomas and Nick Lovegrove at McKinsey & Company and Harvard Kennedy School on the topic of nonlinear careers. Although this sounds fancy, the site itself takes a light-hearted approach to helping you find your path.

To use Paddle, go to www.paddlehr.com/careers and click Get Started. Then, on the top menu bar, click Assessment and start your evaluation.

Answering the questions will take you 10 to 15 minutes. As Paddle recommends, find a quiet place to take this test that is distraction-free. Create an account as soon as you're given the option, so you can go back and reference your results.

When you finish answering the questions, you'll be taken to your results, which you can always access by logging in and clicking Assessment. You can see my results in Figure 3-2.

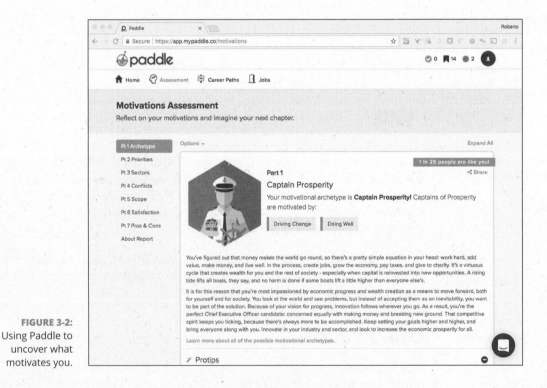

FIGURE 3-2:
Using Paddle to uncover what motivates you.

In my case, I was classified as a "Captain Prosperity," which means I'm motivated by building wealth but also by driving change and doing good. This meshes well with what I've been doing with my career. I wanted to start my own business, but also do it in a way that has a positive impact on others.

You can scroll through the report to learn about the motivators Paddle has identified for you, as you can see in Part 2 of your report, "Priorities," for example. You can also review tips. I find these helpful because they make you think about what drives you, which helps to determine what you want to do and in turn, what careers you may want to pursue.

As you scroll down, go to Part 3, "Sectors," and click it in the left-hand menu bar. You'll be taken to a page with your primary and secondary sectors. Click each one to learn more about it, and most important, to see sample job titles for that sector, as shown in Figure 3-3.

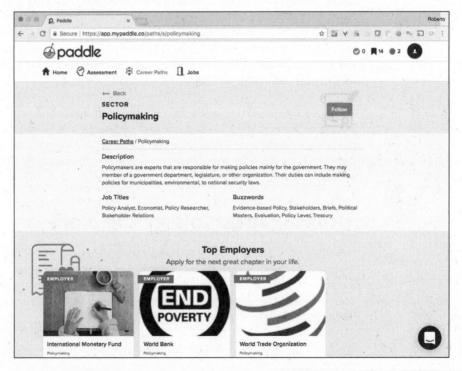

FIGURE 3-3: Sector and job titles recommended by Paddle.

This is actionable data. You can take the sample job titles given and type them into various job boards to get an idea of what jobs in this field entail.

REMEMBER

Gather feedback from assessments like Paddle and ponder the results. Ultimately though, you need to follow your curiosity and passion and do what you want to do, whether it agrees with the results or not.

You can also browse all the other motivational archetypes on Paddle and explore other sectors, not just the ones recommended to you, to get an idea of what's out there.

Getting Insights through Career Discovery Tools

Career discovery tools come in different shapes and packages. The newer ones leverage the power of big data to give you insights into what jobs to pursue. They work by collecting millions of data points from other users on what jobs they have, or activities such as what jobs they click on on job sites, what jobs they view, and what jobs they apply to. Then they do a lot of math behind the scenes to come up with recommendations on what jobs may interest you, based on your own activity on these tools or sites.

If you've ever looked at a job on a job board or applied to one and saw a list of recommended jobs, it's likely that these suggestions were powered by algorithms and a lot of data. So the next time you see some job suggestions on a job board or on your favorite news site, take notice of them. There may be some real science behind them.

Utilizing AfterCollege's Explore

AfterCollege's Explore is one of these career discovery tools that uses big data to help you discover relevant jobs you may not have known about. One of the most common frustrations for college students and recent grads is not knowing what jobs to search for or apply to. This is why the team at AfterCollege created Explore, with new job seekers in mind.

The tool takes your school, major, and grad year to give you a basic set of job recommendations. These suggestions are based on jobs that have been reviewed by other job seekers from your school and major or from similar programs. As you give feedback on jobs you like and dislike, Explore learns from you and keeps tailoring recommended jobs to you.

To use Explore, just follow these steps:

1. **Go to www.aftercollege.com.**

2. **On the home page, under Explore Curated Jobs, enter your college or university, major, and graduation date.**

3. **Click Show Me Jobs.**

    You'll be taken to Explore, as shown in Figure 3-4, which presents you with job or internship recommendations, depending on your graduation year, based on your educational background.

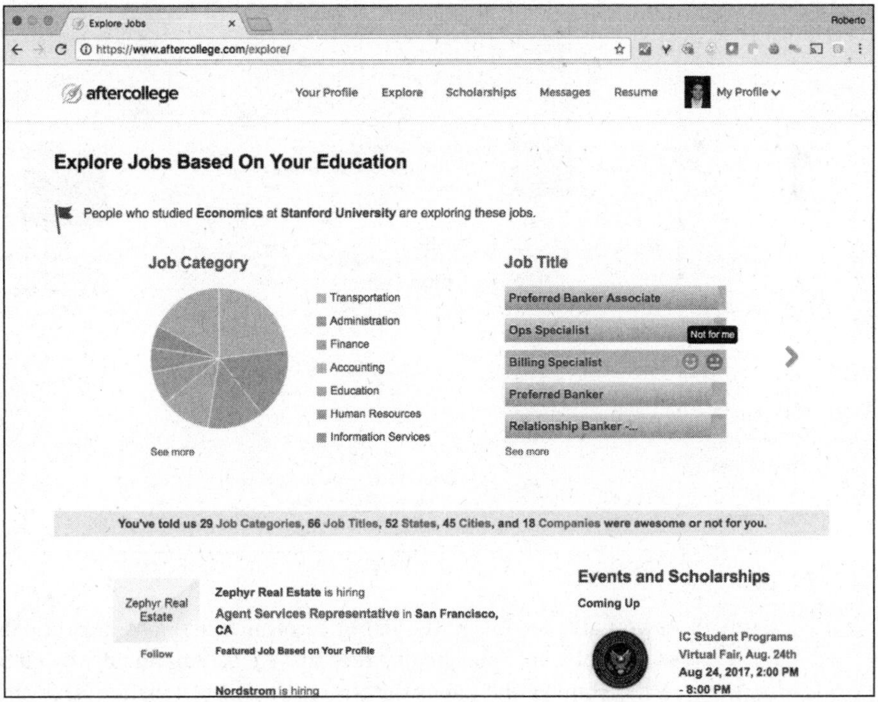

FIGURE 3-4: Job recommendations from AfterCollege's Explore tool.

The first thing you'll notice is a graph of the jobs being recommended to you grouped by job category. You can like or dislike entire categories and Explore will include more or less of those types of jobs.

Initially you may agree with some of the recommendations but not with others. That's because Explore gives you suggestions as best it can based on your background, which it uses to compare you with other similar students who've used Explore and have rated jobs. As you give more feedback, Explore will get more personalized to you and the recommendations will get better and better. As you can see in my case, I've rated 29 job categories, 66 job titles, 45 cities, and 18 companies. The jobs being recommended to me are more appealing as I give more feedback.

You can click on the left of the chart shown in Figure 3-5 and also rate entire states or cities and specific employers.

FIGURE 3-5:
Rating recommended jobs on AfterCollege Explore.

As you give feedback, the list of recommended jobs gets updated. Scroll down to see actual jobs. You can also rate these jobs individually by clicking on the smiley face if you like the job or the frowny face if you dislike it, as shown in Figure 3-5. You can also specify why you like or dislike the job.

TIP

You don't need to register to use Explore. However, if you do, you'll be able to save your feedback and come back to it later. You'll also get recommendations emailed to you.

Leveraging LinkedIn Career Insights

Career Insights by LinkedIn is another great career discovery tool. It takes a different approach than Explore, revealing some very useful information. The tool gives you a good idea of the various career paths that alumni from your school take. LinkedIn takes the millions of profiles it has on its network and allows you to see trends. For example, you can see at which organizations alumni work and what jobs they have. Given the size of LinkedIn's user base, this is the best tool for getting such insight, even better than your alumni association.

Go through these steps to get Career Insights for your school:

1. **Go to www.linkedin.com.**

2. **In the top-left search bar, enter the name of your college or university.**

   You'll land on a LinkedIn page for your school.

3. **Click See Alumni.**

   You're taken to the Career Insights page for your college or university, as shown in Figure 3-6, where you'll see the top cities where alumni live, the top organizations where they work, and the top jobs where they work.

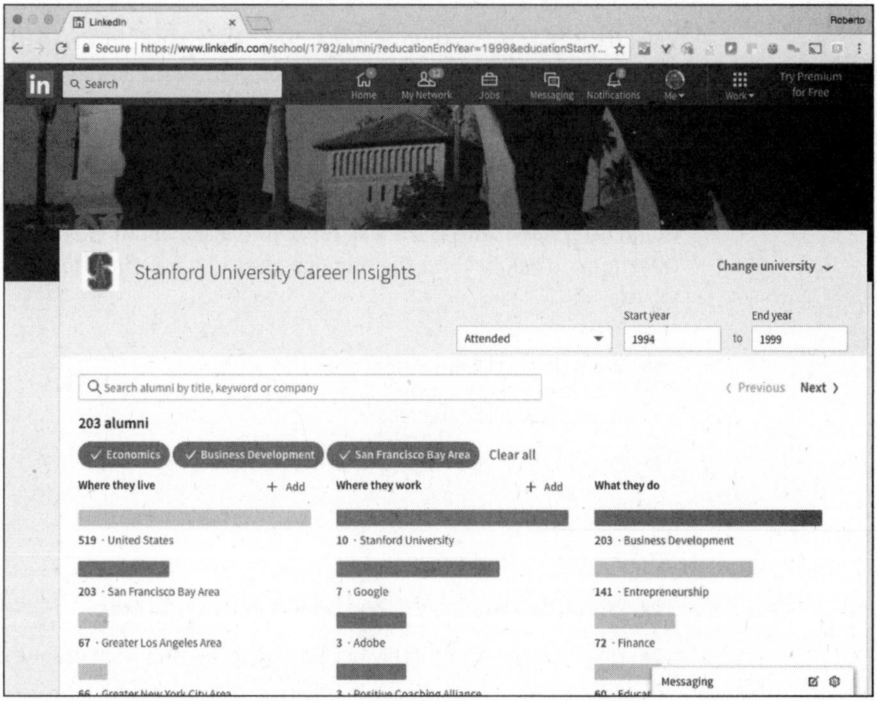

FIGURE 3-6: LinkedIn Career Insights page for a university.

You can narrow the results by graduation year, by major, and by location. You'll be able to see trends on where alumni from various years and majors work. And if you scroll down, you can see actual alumni profiles.

TIP

Reach out to alumni from your school to learn more about their work. Alumni are usually ready and willing to talk to current students.

Identifying Jobs of Interest

Another good way to find out what work you may want to do is to talk to people about their own jobs. This includes talking to friends, classmates, family, alumni, or just about anyone who has a job you think is cool. This method is more traditional and low-tech but it's actually just as effective if not more.

Ask your parents or aunts and uncles if you can tag along and go to their work one day. Best case, you'll discover work you really like. As a worst case, you will have wasted part of a day but found out about jobs you don't like.

Talking to friends about their work

Your friends and classmates are a great starting point in getting an idea of what jobs to explore. Most likely they're in your same shoes and going through the process of finding their first job at the same time or close to when you are.

If you have friends who have just gotten a job or an internship or got one last year, ask them about their experience. This is often referred to as doing an "informational interview" and it's a way for you to learn about what people do in their jobs. Questions to ask beyond the obvious ones of what they do and how they like their job are

>> What do you like the most about your job?

>> What do you like the least?

>> Do you think you'll stay there and for how long?

>> Why?

>> What are you learning?

>> Whom do you report to and what is that person like?

>> Do you have any monthly or quarterly goals and what are they?

This last question is obvious for sales roles and may not be relevant for roles in healthcare, where your obvious goal is patient wellness. But still, this is a general guide of questions you can ask to get an idea of what your friends think of their jobs.

TIP

If you like how a friend describes his job, ask him for an introduction to his employer. Take a look at Chapter 9 to learn more about employee referrals.

Job shadowing

When you were a kid, did your parents ever take you to work for Take Your Child to Work Day? If so, then you're familiar with job shadowing, because the concept is very similar. The idea is to be with someone at work throughout the day, for one or more days, and follow her as she does her job. You may sit with the person at her desk, attend meetings with her, listen in on calls, or hear from her about what she does. This is the best way to learn about a job because you get to see a person first hand doing the work.

You can shadow someone at work through a formal program or take the initiative and do it on your own informally.

Here are some ideas on whom you can approach to job shadow:

>> **University career center:** Visit your school's career center or make an appointment and ask if it has job-shadowing programs set up with any employers. If it does, it can facilitate an introduction to various organizations.

>> **Mentors:** Do you have a mentor who's helped you with your academics or in any other aspect? If so, this is another person you can ask to job shadow. Ask your university career center if it has a mentorship program.

>> **Friends and classmates:** It may be harder for classmates to let you shadow them, especially if they're junior at work. But depending on the field, you should be able to visit a friend or classmate at work to see what he or she does. This tends to be especially true at startups, which tend to have an informal culture where employees are encouraged to bring friends to work, because they can be potential hires.

>> **Family and relatives:** Don't be afraid to ask relatives if you can go see what they do at work. They should be flattered by your request, and you'd be imposing on them for a day at most. That's what family is for, right?

>> **Alumni:** If you find an alum with a job that looks interesting, don't be afraid to reach out to that person via email or LinkedIn. You can also find alumni via your fraternity or sorority, if you belong to one. The worst they can do is ignore you or say "no." Alumni are usually willing to help students from their school.

Writing someone about shadowing

When reaching out to an alum or someone you don't know that well about shadowing him, send a brief email introducing yourself. Here is a simple message template you can customize and use:

> Hello ____,
>
> I'm a current student at _____ majoring in _____. I found you on _____. I'm currently exploring careers to pursue and thought your background and experience were intriguing. Would you be willing to talk to me for a few minutes to talk about your job and what you do? I can give you a call or meet you in person.
>
> Best regards,

Adjust the message as needed. You may not hear back from recipients, but if you do, then schedule calls with them promptly or go visit them. Once you have the call, ask if you can shadow them for part of the day.

Using the Occupational Outlook Handbook

The Bureau of Labor Statistics, part of the U.S. Department of Labor, measures labor market activity in the U.S. economy. It has a lot of current and historical data on the job market, which it makes accessible through its Occupational Outlook Handbook.

The handbook is online and gives you unparalleled access to job descriptions and trends on each occupation. When you have an idea of what jobs you may want to pursue, go to the Occupational Outlook Handbook to research specific jobs, to get an idea of what the work entails, and to see future demand for these types of jobs.

To use the Occupational Outlook Handbook, go to www.bls.gov/ooh. You can browse through the various occupations by navigating through the "occupation groups" on the left-hand menu bar, as shown in Figure 3-7, or you can search for jobs based on various criteria such as median pay, required education, and projected growth rate.

As you find occupations that look interesting, click through to get a detailed description of what the job entails, the educational requirements for the role, and the projected outlook for these types of jobs, as shown in Figure 3-8.

Make note of the tabs on the page where you can click through to see more detail on each attribute for the specific occupation.

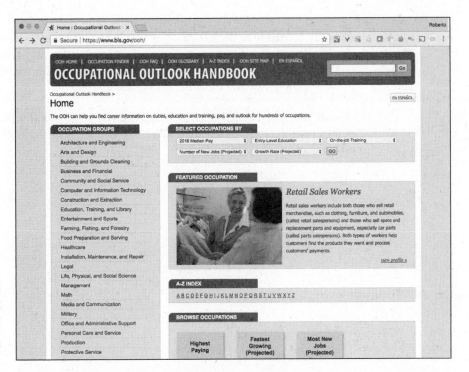

FIGURE 3-7:
Researching careers on the Occupational Outlook Handbook.

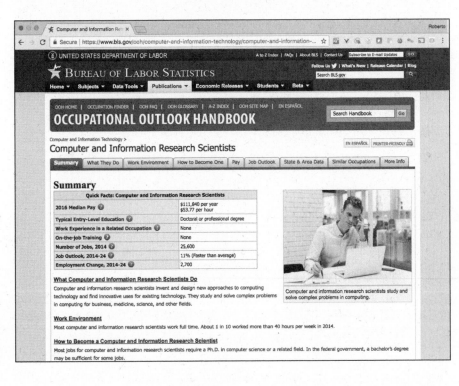

FIGURE 3-8:
Detailed role description on the Occupational Outlook Handbook.

REMEMBER

The only downside to the handbook is that it may not have some of the newer job descriptions or you may have to decipher some job titles to get an idea on the job you're looking for. For example, if you're looking for "data scientist," you'll find it under "Computer and Information Research Scientist."

Overall, the Occupational Outlook Handbook is a great resource that contains a lot of information to give you some guidance. It's also a good example of U.S. tax dollars at work!

2

Starting Your Job Search

Evaluate employers of various sizes and with different training programs to determine which ones are right for you.

Get those around you to help you with your job search by asking for endorsements.

Become familiar with on-campus resources that can support you in finding your first job.

Learn advanced techniques to uncover jobs on search engines and job boards.

Create a professional online presence and clean up your social media so employers see what you want them to see.

Chapter **4**

Researching Employers

Finding the right employer is just as important as finding the right job. Most people jump straight into the job search without paying much attention to the type of employer that will make them happiest. Employers come in all shapes and sizes, and each has its own culture and traits that make it unique. It's important that you do some basic research on the various types of employers.

In this chapter, you evaluate the pros and cons of working for large and small companies. You also learn about different types of employers, such as startups and government agencies.

You also make a mental list of the benefits that are important to you. For example, some employers offer training programs for new college graduates. These programs are great as you begin your career, and they can make all the difference in the world when it comes to job satisfaction.

A great job is even better if you work at a great company. In this chapter, I fill you in on resources you can use to get a glimpse of the inner workings of employers that interest you. For example, what do employees say about their company? And how long do they stay there? Where do successful alumni from your school go to work? These are some of the questions you'll be able to answer after reading this chapter.

Comparing Large and Small Employers

Landing a job at the right organization or company will have a significant impact on the start of your career. Although there are many factors to consider in an employer, company size is one of the most important aspects because it correlates to other attributes. For example, large employers tend to have more resources. Specifically, these resources can take the form of learning tools, tuition reimbursement, and infrastructure to help you acquire new skills and knowledge to help you do your job. What you learn at your new job will also help you throughout your career. Large employers also tend to have more established processes in place which cover how you build new products and how you introduce these products to the market. Promotions and pay increases are also often guided by these processes.

REMEMBER

Large employers have more people, which means more opportunities to collaborate with other individuals. This also opens up the door for you to make lateral moves to other groups within the organization.

On the other hand, large employers, because of their size, may also have their disadvantages. With more employees in an organization, there may also be more bureaucracy, since you need to check with more people to do certain things. At a large employer, your job is often more defined, which is good if you like structure, but also restrictive in terms of how far you can stray from your responsibilities in order to try new things. The structure and processes of a large organization can be a blessing and a guide to help you navigate your job. But it can also be frustrating if you're used to moving fast and not having to deal with process.

Small employers have their advantages. Often, small companies lack the processes of larger ones. This means you have more flexibility and you can get things done faster. At a small organization, you also tend to have more of an impact. This is because in an organization with fewer people, your contributions are felt more. Furthermore, you're often able to go outside your defined role at a small employer and try new things.

On the flip side, small companies sometimes lack the resources of large ones. This means you may not always get the latest technology or software for your job (some large companies give employees free iPhones or iPads). But again, the flexibility and freedom to stray from your prescribed role may be worth forgoing free gadgets.

Evaluating the advantages of a large company

The benefits that come with working for a large employer are many, and they vary in importance. Here are some of the pros of working for a large company.

Teams

More employees means more teams. As part of a team, you get to interact with others who will help you gain knowledge. At the same time, you get to interact with other teams. For example, if you're a project manager in a team of project managers, you'll get to learn from some of the senior members on your team. And as a project manager, you're probably working with cross-functional teams of engineers, programmers, and finance people within the organization. You may also work with client teams.

All these interactions do two things for you:

>> You'll meet people from whom you'll learn.

>> You'll expand your professional network, which will come in handy as you eventually look for your next job or project.

Learning resources

Although not exclusive to large companies, many large employers tend to have educational assistance and tuition reimbursement programs. Employers offer these programs in order to retain employees, attract new ones, and ensure workers keep their skills up to date.

An example of an employer offering tuition reimbursement is Procter & Gamble. As of the writing of this book, it reimburses up to 80 percent of tuition and qualifying fees on courses that relate to your current or future assignment at the company, with a cap of $40,000 over the span of your employment with the company. Children's National Health System, based in Washington, D.C., is another organization that provides educational assistance. It offers assistance after six months of employment and your education must lead to a degree.

REMEMBER

One thing to look out for when considering an employer that offers tuition reimbursement are the repayment terms. Often times, when you leave an employer before a certain amount of time, you may have to repay part or all of your tuition assistance.

Benefits

Benefits are prevalent at most employers. But when you join a large organization, these benefits tend to be richer. Retirement saving and investment plans are one of these benefits. At companies, the most common benefit is the 401(k). At nonprofit institutions, these plans are called 403(b) plans, and at government agencies, they are referred to as 457(b) plans. These non-glamorous names come from the sections of the U.S. Internal Revenue Service code where the programs are defined.

The advantage of these plans is that you get to save money for retirement from funds subtracted directly from your paycheck, before taxes. This is a big benefit in itself because it's rare to be able to use pre-tax money for savings. The higher your tax rate, the more you can benefit from these plans.

Again, many employers offer retirement plans. But large companies tend to offer better matching for your contributions. Yes, this is what you think it is. For every dollar you contribute to your 401(k) plan, the employer will contribute a matching amount as well, up to a certain point, usually up to 6 percent of your pre-tax income.

For more on 401(k) plans, check out Chapter 18.

Perks

Companies also tend to offer special perks to outdo other employers in order to retain employees. For example, companies like Salesforce.com, based in San Francisco, offers a free iPhone to qualifying employees, with a fully paid call plan. Other employees tend to offer other gadgets. For example, LinkedIn, at one point, gave free iPads to all its employees. Google, which is one of the largest and most well regarded employers in the world, offers free lunch and access to a full gym to its employees.

These perks can also include free transportation to and from work. In the San Francisco Bay Area, which has a lot of traffic congestion and not enough transportation between cities, large companies like Apple, Google, and Genentech offer bus service from various points in San Francisco to the South Bay and to Silicon Valley. These buses are often more comfortable than public buses and they include free Wi-Fi.

Brand recognition

Large organizations, especially consumer-facing ones, tend to have good recognizable brand names. Examples of such employers include Google, Apple, and Facebook, which touch most people's daily lives. Other brand names include companies like Oracle and Salesforce.com, which sell to other businesses. The you have government agencies like the National Security Agency (NSA) and NASA. Working for organizations such as these provides you with a good brand name that you can put on your résumé or profile, and can help you down the line as you look for your next job.

TIP

Working for a brand-name employer can help get you in the door of a future employer.

Considering the advantages of a small company

Working for a small employer can have its advantages. It all depends on what you're looking for in your job. Here are some of the perks that come with being part of a smaller team.

More freedom

This means having the flexibility to stray from your daily job routine and explore new tasks and projects. At a larger company, roles are typically well defined. For example, you may be hired as a software engineer to work on a certain feature for a specific product. Working on another product or feature may not be in the cards for you if there is already another person or group working on that other product. At a smaller company, however, where there aren't as many engineers, you may be able to work on, let's say, the Android version of your company's mobile app, and then also tinker with the iOS version of the app.

At AfterCollege, my 40-person company, for example, we've had software engineers work in different programming languages depending on the project. In one instance, one of the software engineers wanted to learn more about machine learning, and moved from programming to being one of our lead machine learning and data analytics engineers. The ability to try and learn new things, and to move to new areas as the need arises, is one of the pluses of working for a smaller employer for this person.

Less bureaucracy

Fewer people at an organization also means fewer layers of managers to get approvals and fewer people to check with in order to get things done. Let's say you're working in sales at a small company and you identify some new customer relationship management (CRM) software that can make your job and those of your colleagues easier. At a small organization, you may have a direct relationship to the head of sales or even the president of the company. If you present your case well enough, you may be able to get what you need fairly quickly. This could be days or weeks, compared to months, years, or never at a large company. Therefore, with less bureaucracy tends to come speed.

Larger impact

Being part of a smaller team also means you carry more weight on your shoulders, and your contributions are felt more throughout the organization. For example, if you're part of a four-person sales team, your sales quota may account for a quarter of the organization's revenue. Your ability to exceed sales goals will have a significant positive effect on the company. Whereas missing your sales goal can have an adverse effect on the company. In another instance, you could be one of a handful of software developers building the next great artificial intelligence–driven chat bot for a company. Your ability to work with a small team to build a great product and quickly take it to market can mean your company reaches profitability or gets its next round of venture funding. Having such a level of impact on an organization can be stressful for some people, but it can also be extremely rewarding.

More visibility

If you like being recognized and acknowledged for your work, a small company may be for you. This is because it's harder to hide in an organization with fewer people. Your contributions carry more weight. And they'll most likely be seen all the way up to the top, by the CEO of your company or the executive director of your nonprofit. So, if you're looking to do good work and you want it to show, you'll be able to do so more easily in a smaller setting.

Access to decision makers

Closely related to being more visible is having access to those making the decisions. Smaller organizations have fewer layers, which means you're more likely to interact with the executives in the organization, including vice presidents, founders, and the CEO. These are people you can learn from!

Knowing if a startup is right for you

Startups are good examples of small organizations. However, you can also find large startups like Uber, Lyft, and Airbnb. These companies started small but because of their success or large amount of investment they've received, they've experienced hyper-growth. Regardless of their size, work at these startups often has the following benefits.

Stock options

Stock options give you the potential for a big payday and are a common benefit awarded at startup companies. These options allow you to buy stock in the company at a certain price per share, usually a low price. As the value of the company grows, so does the value of its shares. And because you have the option to buy shares at a predetermined low price, this is where you can make some money.

For example, you join a startup and you get 10,000 stock options in the company. The exercise price, or *strike price*, of these options is $1 per share, meaning you have the option to buy shares at a dollar each. At some point in the future, lets say the company gets bought or it goes on the stock market via an initial public offering (IPO). The price of the stock is then $10 per share. In this hypothetical scenario, you've made $9 per share, or $90,000, since you have options for 10,000 shares.

That's a pretty nice payday. One thing to note is that stock options usually have vesting schedules. This means you can't join a startup, get options, and then leave the following week with your options. Vesting schedules are usually four years in length and allow you to exercise a fourth of your stock options each year until fully vested. Options usually also carry what's called a *cliff*, which means you need to stay with the company for at least six months to a year before you can exercise any of your options.

REMEMBER

Although stock options can provide a great payday at some point, this is not usually the case. You hear about the great success stories like Apple, Google, and Facebook where some early employees became multi-millionaires because of their options. In reality, only a handful of startups hit it big. The vast majority of them either fail or achieve modest success. You rarely hear about these companies in the news.

For more on stock options, check out Chapter 18.

Faster work pace

The work at a startup can be rewarding, because you're usually disrupting a market or working on some cool innovative product. But this often means you're working on rushed deadlines and at a faster pace than what you may see in a typical organization. Because startups are disrupting markets, speed is key in order to launch a product, grow market share, and stay ahead of the competition.

More stress

Startups often follow a make-or-break strategy, where they invest heavily on a strategy with the hope of success, but with the risk of failing. Such failure can take the form of the company running out of money and having to do layoffs or shutting down. Because startups usually have no revenue but need cash to pay employees to build products, many startups rely on investors to get off the ground and fuel growth. This investment usually comes in stages, or *rounds,* and the company raises these rounds by selling shares in the company as it reaches certain product, usage, or revenue milestones. As you can imagine, there is tremendous pressure to meet these milestones in order to get to the next round of funding. You'll need to decide whether you're someone who thrives under pressure or buckles when you get stressed.

Less work–life balance

The concept of having a balance between your work life and personal life is a fantasy in most startups. Because of the pace of the work, the deadlines and the stress involved, you'll most likely be working odd and late hours. If you have a family and value spending time with them, you'll see less of them. If you have hobbies that you enjoy, be prepared to spend less time on them. Your job at a startup will most likely demand a good chunk of your waking time. Not only that, but it may also take a toll mentally and emotionally.

Startups change the world. Just think about companies like Google, which is making information accessible to everyone, or Tesla, which is working to bring electric vehicles to everyone and reduce pollution. You'll make an impact, do exciting work, and most likely learn a lot — regardless of whether the startup succeeds or fails.

Best of all, you'll also have the potential to make a lot of money. But this comes at a cost, because it takes away time from loved ones and from the activities you enjoy doing. If you're single and you have few commitments, working at a startup can be a great opportunity. Just make sure you evaluate the pros and cons.

Learning about startups on Crunchbase

Make sure you do your homework when looking at a potential employer. The same goes for a startup. Crunchbase offers insights on most startup companies including who invested in them, the products they offer, and related news information.

To look up a company, just go to www.crunchbase.com, type the company name in the search box at the top of the page, and scroll down to see information on the company's investors, how much money it has raised, its product, and the people involved in the startup.

TIP

Pay attention to how much money the company has raised. It gives you an idea of how well funded the startup is and shows who is backing the company. If you see prominent investor names listed, this is usually a good thing.

Working for a nonprofit

Nonprofits are another way to go when considering where to look for your first job. Teach for America and the Peace Corps are examples of great organizations where you can make a positive impact while also gaining experience. Nonprofits abound, and they include large organizations like the Bill & Melinda Gates Foundation, which works to improve healthcare and to eliminate extreme poverty. They also include smaller regional trade associations such as the Northern California HR Association, which works to advance the human resources profession. Here are some of the factors to consider when looking at nonprofits:

>> **Social impact:** Nonprofits are usually mission driven. If you're passionate about a certain issue such as climate change, education, or healthcare, a nonprofit can give you the ability to apply your skills and energy to a worthy cause.

>> **Prestige:** Working at organizations like the Peace Corps gives you valuable experience that you can list on your résumé. Employers look highly on candidates who've done assignments at these types of organizations. It shows that you're mission driven and that you're not afraid of hard work.

>> **Hands-on training:** Organizations like the Peace Corps and Teach for America offer intense training. But afterward, you're mostly on your own. Working at nonprofits such as these gives you the opportunity to learn while doing the work.

>> **Less support:** Not all nonprofits have the support structures in place to help you do your job. In fact, most of them typically look for people with experience or some specific skill set so they can start contributing to the organization soon after they join. Be aware that if you're joining a nonprofit, you'll need to take the lead on your own professional development.

>> **Less pay:** Nonprofits typically pay less than private-sector jobs. This is because nonprofits are not profit driven and they tend to rely on donations and grants for their funding. As a result, they may not be able to pay you a market rate. Nonprofit experience can be valuable as you start your career. But also keep in mind that it's hard work that is not often rewarded monetarily. The work itself tends to be the reward.

Finding Employers with New-Grad Programs

A number of large employers rely heavily on new college graduates and entry-level talent to staff their businesses. As a result, they offer new-grad programs that teach new hires about the company culture, arm them with skills that are relevant to the job, and provide experience. These programs are ideal if you're looking for a structured environment that will give you solid guidance as you embark on your career. Here are some examples of the types of new-grad programs available.

Rotation programs

Rotation programs are great because they let you try out various roles at a company before committing to one. Think of it as a "shopping before buying" for your career. Intel, for example, offers rotation programs in different fields such as finance, human resources, information technology, and sales and marketing. You can try a role every 18 to 36 months.

You can usually apply for rotation programs and learn more about them via the employer's website.

You can find employer rotation programs on job sites and you can also go to Google and do a simple search yourself. Just search for *new-grad rotation programs.*

Nursing programs

Are you interested in becoming a nurse or in the process of getting your nursing degree? When you complete your degree, usually a bachelor of science in nursing (BSN) or higher, you'll need to gain some hands-on experience. Find a hospital or healthcare organization that offers a nursing new-grad or nurse-residency program. These programs usually last one year, and you get paired up with a senior nurse, called a *preceptor.* You'll get exposed to the various aspects of nursing, and you can choose from specific specialty areas.

TIP

Employers that offer nursing new-grad residency programs are usually well-established hospitals and include prominent names such as UCLA Health, Children's National Health System, and Cedars-Sinai.

You can find out about new-grad programs at your school and through your classmates. Many hospitals visit local nursing schools to promote their residency programs. You can also find out about these programs by searching on Google or entry-level job sites like AfterCollege.com. Just search for *nursing new grad.*

TIP

Some sites require the use of quotation marks; others don't. Try both to see what yields the best results.

Sales programs

When people think of sales, they usually think of car salesmen or door-to-door salesmen. These are just two types of sales out of many. Sales and sales-related jobs are among the most prevalent in the labor market. If you like sales and know how to do it well, you can go into a variety of industries and have a very lucrative career. For example, you can work in pharmaceutical sales, enterprise software sales (selling software packages to large companies), or selling subscriptions or software over the phone.

Oracle, a large cloud-based software company, offers a multi-week sales training program for its new college hires. The program trains you on new sales-related skills each week and involves working in teams with a class of other recent graduates. You also get to shadow an experienced salesperson before you start your job. On the website of a good sales training program, you should be able to find videos, testimonials, and detailed information about what the program entails.

TIP

Having good sales skills opens opportunities in various fields. You can couple these sales skills with knowledge of a specific industry or product to make a good income.

Be wary of sales training programs that don't offer to pay you or that offer commission only opportunities. Yes, the company may be investing in training you, but you're also investing your time in it. Established programs will pay you a base salary on top of commission. Ask your classmates and friends who've gone into sales for advice. You can also look online on job sites or on Google by searching for *+college +graduate +sales +training.*

Identifying Employers of Interest

Now that you have an idea of what kind of job to pursue and what type of employer to work for, it's time to do some investigation. Your next step is to figure out what it's like to work for the particular employer(s) that interest you. We're lucky to live in a time where you can easily access such information, which includes insights on company culture, employee tenure, and sentiment. Services like Glassdoor and LinkedIn provide a treasure-trove of information related to an organization's inner workings.

Gauging employee morale on Glassdoor

Glassdoor is a large Internet job board that is best known for its reviews on companies conducted by current and past employees. These reviews rate aspects of an employer including the workplace, fellow team members, and the CEO of the organization. You can scroll through the review section for a specific employers and read detailed accounts from current and former employees. Just go to www.glassdoor.com, click Company Reviews, and type the company name in the search box. When you get to the company's page, click the Reviews tab.

TIP

Sort the reviews by date, from most recent to oldest, because this gives you the best picture of what's happening now at the particular employer. A lot of bad reviews from three years ago may be irrelevant if the reviews for the past year have been stellar. Conversely, if the company had great reviews in the past and has bad reviews currently, you may want to avoid the company.

TIP

It typically takes a company about a year to go from being good to bad or bad to good. So focus on reviews for the past 12 months.

Gleaning employee insights on LinkedIn

LinkedIn is a great resource for getting good insights about a particular employer. For instance, you can see who works there and whom you may know, whether it's directly or via a friend or colleague. Note that this only works if you're connected to other people on LinkedIn and if any of them work at the employer of interest.

To find people on LinkedIn, just go to www.linkedin.com, type the employer name in the search box, and go to the employer page. You'll see a list of your connections on the right side of the page. Click the Connections link to see a detailed list of people you know.

On that same page, you can also see people you know who previously worked for the employer. Simply uncheck the employer's name under the Current Companies filter and check it again under the Past Companies filter. You may be able to get more candid feedback from contacts who previously worked for the organization.

You can use LinkedIn to gain other insights on an employer as well. For example, you can see if there's anyone from your school who works there. On the employer page, click the See All *Company* Employees on LinkedIn link. On the right, scroll down to the Schools filter, and select your school. You'll see current and past employees of that company who went to your school.

TIP

You can click the various user profiles to see the job titles that individuals hold. You can also see how long they've been at the company. These insights help you get a good glimpse of what kind of people work at the company, the titles they hold, and how long they stay.

Chapter 5

Getting Ready to Search for a Job

A s you begin to look for your first job, start thinking of those around you who can help you in your search. You most likely have an existing support network that you didn't know you had. Classmates, family, friends, and even some of your professors can help you become aware of opportunities and make introductions.

These individuals can also serve as good references for you. In this chapter, you learn how to approach your network and ask them to recommend you. You also gain knowledge of tools and techniques to do this more easily.

Leverage social media to let your contacts know that you're looking for a job and get a walk-through on how to do this. This chapter fills you in on the resources typically available to you through your school and its career center. For example, most schools organize job fairs and networking events for students looking for jobs and internships. These are great opportunities to connect with prospective employers.

Enlisting Assistance from Your Network

Friends, classmates, and teachers are often cited by students as being among the most effective contacts for job searching. These individuals form part of your network, and you should definitely lean on them to find your first job. Your classmates and friends are most likely in the same boat you're in — they're also looking for their first job. So during the job search process, compare notes with them. Make them aware of any job leads. Share best practices you've learned. In return, your friends may do the same.

TIP

Identify some friends or classmates who are also looking for their first jobs and treat your journey as you would a study group. Help each other with doing research on employers, interview preparation, and figuring out what to wear.

Networking with LinkedIn

LinkedIn is as effective as the number of contacts you have. The larger your number of online connections, the louder your megaphone for letting people know about career and educational updates.

When you've established a LinkedIn profile (see Chapter 7), LinkedIn can help you in two simple ways:

>> **Be found.** By having a profile with some basic information such as your school and major, you're likely to be found by recruiters who are looking for entry-level candidates.

>> **Tell people you're looking.** LinkedIn allows you to update your headline to announce things to your network. This small and simple action has high impact, because it lets your LinkedIn network know you're looking for work. And you never know — someone can stumble upon an opportunity that is relevant to you and make you aware of it. Always let your contacts know that you're exploring opportunities.

People on LinkedIn typically don't announce that they're looking for a job, out of fear that their current employer will find out. But in your case, because this is your first job, it's not an issue. Take advantage and announce your search.

To announce on LinkedIn that you're looking for a job, update your profile headline and summary. Do this by following these steps:

1. Go to www.linkedin.com and make sure you're logged in.

2. On the top menu bar, scroll to the right and click Me to bring up a menu bar.

3. **Click View Profile.**

4. **Click the pencil icon on the right side of your profile.**

   This will bring up an edit screen (see Figure 5-1).

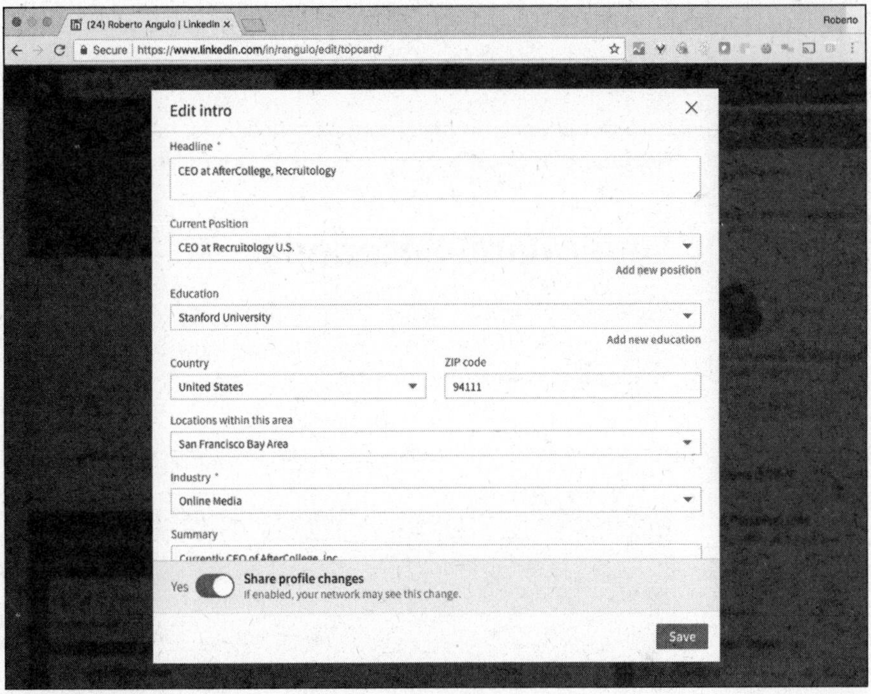

FIGURE 5-1:
Updating your
headline and
summary on
LinkedIn.

5. **Next to Share Profile Changes, change the switch to Yes.**

   This ensures that your contacts will be aware of the updates you'll make.

Update your headline and summary. For your headline, you can use something along these lines:

   Stanford University economics student looking for internship

The headline should be one line; it should describe what you do and what you're looking for.

Keep the summary to three lines and add some specific skills. Avoid using adjectives like *enthusiastic* or phrases like *eager to learn*. These are more fluff than real information. Keep it focused on specific skills and attributes you bring to an employer. A good example of a summary can be something like this:

Majoring in economics at Stanford.

Knowledgeable in Microsoft Excel and SQL, and experienced in developing financial models.

Enjoy working with data to glean insights that help solve business problems.

REMEMBER

Pack some specific skills and knowledge in your profile summary so when a recruiter glances at your profile, the summary and headline will catch her eye.

Leveraging Facebook

Use Facebook in the same way as LinkedIn to let your friends know that you're looking for a job. You can do this easily by creating a status update and making it public, as shown in Figure 5-2.

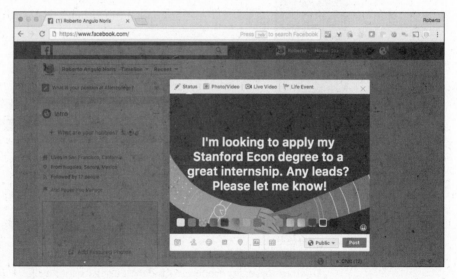

FIGURE 5-2:
Letting your friends on Facebook know you're looking for a job.

TIP

Complete your Facebook profile by adding your school, major, and any previous internship experience you've had. More employers are using Facebook to look for talent, so the more information you have, the more likely you are to be found.

Here are some ways to make your update stand out:

>> **Make it public.** By default, updates appear only to your friends. Make this one public so everyone sees it.

>> **Add a background.** Facebook now lets you add a background to your updates. Doing this will make your update stand out.

>> **Add a link to your professional profile.** If you have a LinkedIn or AfterCollege profile, add a link to it in your update.

Going to alumni events

Alumni are an effective channel that can help you get a job. But how do you connect with them? You can do it online via LinkedIn, but you can also do it with a more personal touch like the following:

>> **Alumni events:** Annual reunions tend to bring alumni back to campus. Check with your alumni association or career center about any upcoming mixers for students and alumni.

>> **Alumni houses:** Some of the big universities tend to have regional alumni offices or houses around the world. If this is the case with your school, check with the local representative to see if they have any opportunities to connect with alumni.

>> **Fraternity and sorority events:** Not everyone was in a fraternity or sorority in college, but if you were, then this is a network of individuals who can also help you. Don't be shy about asking for help or leads.

>> **Tailgaters:** These are also a great opportunity to meet alumni. Although they're social events, you can take the opportunity to get to know people and ask them about what they do. You can mention casually that you're looking for opportunities.

TIP

Do you belong to any alumni email lists or groups? If so, send your résumé along with a detailed note asking if anyone knows of opportunities available for someone with your school and major.

Talking to your teachers and professors

Professors and teachers are among the most influential people who can help you in your career. Professors are obviously knowledgeable in the subject matter they teach. They know their field and they also tend to know people working in their field. Because of this, they're in a good position to help you with leads and introductions.

TIP

When you think of professors, also add your teachers, teaching assistants, department head, academic advisor, or thesis advisor into this category of people who can help you.

Professors are usually busy teaching classes and doing research, and it's not in their job description to help students find jobs. Most of the professors I've spoken to, though, feel a sense of responsibility to help their students. They want their students to do well when they graduate.

Here are some ways your professors can help you:

>> **Identifying promising jobs:** Faculty tend to be experts in their field and industry. Because of this, they're likely to know what jobs are out there that are relevant to you and your major. For example, your economics professor may be able to tell you about policy jobs at government agencies or analyst jobs at companies that she has worked with before.

>> **Pointing you to interesting organizations:** Professors can also point you to employers that hire people with your educational background. Many professors consult for other organizations while also teaching. In my case, for example, I had professors who worked for the World Bank, the International Monetary Fund, and for companies like Hewlett Packard and Google. If you have the opportunity, ask a professor what kind of work she does for these organizations and ask if she knows of any relevant entry-level opportunities within these firms.

>> **Making introductions:** Not many faculty do this, but in some cases, especially if you're working on your master's degree or PhD, professors can introduce you to people in their industry with whom they've worked. If you have a good relationship with a teacher or professor, ask him to introduce you to employers in his network. Professors who advise PhD students tend to stay in touch with their students after they've graduated. And these grads tend to go back to their professors when they're looking to hire recent grads.

>> **Sharing job leads:** When I was in college, my most interesting job and internship leads came from my professors and department administrators. Savvy employers know that the best way to reach students from your school and major is to contact your department. So if you get an email from a professor, teaching assistant, or department administrator about a job or an internship, take notice. These opportunities are typically very relevant and have been targeted by the employer to students with your educational profile.

>> **Giving you an endorsement:** Ask early. Some professors, especially the ones who teach a large number of students, don't give recommendations because, if they do it for one student, they need to do it for everyone. Still, if you work closely with a professor and she knows you, ask her for a letter of

REMEMBER

recommendation. You can also ask her for permission to give her name and contact information as a reference to potential employers.

Don't get discouraged if you ask a professor for help and she turns you down. Not all professors are able to help. Some are busy and have so many students that they set a policy of not giving recommendations or making introductions.

Getting help from family and friends

Your family and friends are most likely the people who know you the best. They have a good idea of what you're good at doing and your top qualities. They also know where you need to improve. This makes them good at judging what jobs may be relevant and interesting to you. Ask them for help in keeping an eye open for jobs that could be a good fit for you.

Here are other ways your friends can help you:

>> **Getting an internship, co-op, or temporary job.** A friend, relative, or friend of the family may hesitate to get you a full-time job simply because of the connection. This is fair — nepotism is seen as a negative thing and your friend or relative may get in trouble at work. With internships or temporary jobs, especially if they're unpaid, this shouldn't be an issue.

Internships and co-ops are temporary, usually lasting two to three months. Because of the short duration, employers tend to be less strict on how these hires are made. In fact, it's often unspoken that friends tend to help other friends by giving internships to their relatives. Don't be shy about leveraging your connections or asking relatives to leverage their connections for an internship. If you do well in your internship, everyone wins. If this is not the case, it was only a two- to three-month stint.

TIP

When leveraging a family connection or friend to get a job, reach out to the employer yourself and don't rely on your connection to do it for you. This shows the employer that you're proactive and you take the initiative. You'll make a good impression.

>> **Employee referrals:** A simple referral, even if not an endorsement, often helps to get you through the door and to secure an interview. Larger employers often pay employees a referral fee for recommending someone who ultimately gets hired and stays with the organization for some period of time, normally three to six months.

If you have friends who work at an employer of interest, ask them if they can submit your résumé or add a note with the recruiter that you've applied for the job. They'll be doing you a favor and they may also earn a bonus.

Obtaining Recommendations

One of the advantages of being a first-time job seeker is that employers most likely won't ask you for references. This is because they know you haven't had any previous employment. Nonetheless, some employers may ask you for some references.

To paraphrase a popular saying, it's better to have the references and not need them than to need them and not have them. You're also better off asking for references early on in your job-seeking quest to get this out of the way. This way, you're not scrambling later on trying to get endorsements on short notice while an employer is waiting for them before it can give you an offer.

TIP

Start making a list of past employers, teachers, and classmates whom you'll ask to serve as references or to give you endorsements.

Securing past employer recommendations

You've most likely had internships or a part-time job in the past, or you've done some volunteer work. If so, start asking some of your past employers if they can act as references. You can also ask them for recommendations ahead of time, even if you're not sure your prospective employer will need them. It's up to you.

TIP

Past bosses often move on to other organizations. If all your prospective employer needs is to verify past employers, give it the main number for the organization. If you or your employer needs a recommendation or reference, track down your former boss and reach out to her.

Writing someone for a recommendation

You may have a great relationship with your former boss where it's easy for you to ask for a reference or recommendation. Either way, be polite and ask early enough. Also, be ready to thank the person for any reference or recommendation, whether or not you get the job.

Here's a simple note you can send to your former employer, via email or via LinkedIn, asking for a good word from him:

Hello, ____.

I hope you're doing well. I'm in the process of looking for a job and I'd like to list you as a reference. I had a great experience working with you and learned a lot. I'd like to share your name and contact information with prospective employers.

Please confirm this is okay and let me know what email or phone number I can provide as contact information.

Thank you very much, and take care,

Your Name

If you need a reference letter, definitely ask for it early in the process. They take time to write, and you want to make sure you give the person enough time to write you a good letter. Here's an example of how you can make the request. Fill in the blanks appropriately. Make sure you provide a deadline of when you need the letter, and most important, always be courteous. Also, add details on the job you're pursuing and a link to the job description if you have one. This will help the person craft the letter.

Hello, _____.

I hope you're doing well! I'm in the process of looking for a job, and I'd like to ask you for a letter of recommendation. I know you're busy, and I appreciate your help. The deadline for the letter is _____ and you can send it to _____.

The opportunity I'm considering is a _____ role with _____. My job would entail doing _____.

I've attached the job description to help you understand the role.

A good word from you will definitely help my prospects in securing this job. Your letter can briefly describe the work I did for you, some of my best qualities, and how you think I can do well in this role.

If you can do this, please let me know. I really appreciate it! Also, please let me know if I can do anything to make it easier for you to write the letter.

Thank you in advance and best regards,

Your Name

TIP

Be ready to provide the writer of your letter with some bullet points of items to include in the letter. This can include some of your strengths and specific contributions. You may also need to write the letter for that person.

Approaching teachers for recommendations

Professors typically don't do recommendations unless they know you well enough. If you have a professor you work with or an advisor, she should be willing to write you a letter. You can also approach a faculty advisor of a student group if you belonged to one, especially if you were in a leadership position.

Here are some things to remember when asking a professor for a recommendation:

>> **Ask early.** Do it prior to finals or midterms, when your professor will most likely be inundated with grading papers or exams.

>> **Consider teaching assistants.** If your professor is unable to write a letter, ask the teaching assistant. A professor is more prestigious, but a teaching assistant's recommendation is better than no recommendation at all.

>> **Write your own letter.** In some cases, you may be asked to write the letter yourself, for the professor, and then hand it to him so he can add the finishing touches. If you get asked to write your own letter, don't be bummed. It's normal and it just means the individual is busy, but he wants to help you.

Crafting your own recommendation letter

If you're asked to write your own letter, here's a sample letter you can customize and use:

To whom it may concern,

It is with pleasure that I recommend YOUR NAME HERE for _____ role at _____.

As I understand, the opportunity entails doing _____

_____.

YOUR NAME HERE is an ideal candidate for this position. While he/she was a student in my _____ class/group, he/she showed great aptitude in _____ and performed well, obtaining one of the top scores in the class. The work involved working in a group, and YOUR NAME HERE was able to work well and collaboratively as part of a team. His/her fellow team members often went to YOUR NAME HERE for assistance and relied on him/her for feedback.

YOUR NAME HERE showed mastery of the subject matter and was always willing to help others.

I believe YOUR NAME HERE's work style, ability to master difficult concepts, and willingness to help others provide him/her with the skills necessary to succeed in any endeavor he/she sets his/her mind to. I would, therefore, appreciate any consideration you can give YOUR NAME HERE for this position.

Sincerely,

TIP

When writing your own letter, provide the document to the person recommending you in a file format where she can easily make edits (such as Microsoft Word).

Be sure to include the following components in the letter:

>> **Role and responsibilities:** Include the job that you're applying to and details about what the job entails.

>> **Organization:** Include the organization that you're applying to.

>> **Accomplishments:** Include any of your specific accomplishments or results you achieved that the recommender can point to in his letter.

>> **Skill sets:** Include any skills that are relevant to the job you're applying to that the recommender will also be willing to write about.

Requesting endorsements via LinkedIn

LinkedIn makes it easy for you to ask for recommendations. When someone recommends you, her endorsement appears as part of your profile. Recruiters who look at your profile will usually look to see if you have any recommendations. Not having them doesn't hurt you, but having them definitely adds to the appeal of your profile and makes you stand out.

To get recommended on LinkedIn, follow these steps:

1. Go to www.linkedin.com.

2. In the upper-left search bar of the screen, enter the name of the person whom you would like to ask for a recommendation.

3. Click the three dots toward the top of the person's profile and select Request a Recommendation from the drop-down menu.

4. Select the relationship you have with the recommender and the role you had, as shown in Figure 5-3.

On the next screen, you'll be able to enter a message for the person. Make sure you personalize this message and include detail about yourself, your interactions with the person, and any specific aspects that you would like the recommender to mention.

When you receive a recommendation on LinkedIn, you can decide if you want to accept it. You can also keep it private for now and make it public at a later point.

FIGURE 5-3:
Asking for a
recommendation
on LinkedIn.

Recommenders on LinkedIn need to be LinkedIn members, and you need to be connected to them. Many people in academia are on LinkedIn, but not all. I address a way to get around this in the next section.

REMEMBER

Asking for recommendations via AfterCollege

You can also ask for recommendation on AfterCollege, similar to how you can on LinkedIn. With AfterCollege, though, the recommender doesn't have to be a member and you can ask anyone, as long as you have the person's email address.

Recommendations will appear in your AfterCollege profile, which you can make public and share with employers. You can add a link to your public profile on your résumé or send the link to employers directly.

To ask for a recommendation on AfterCollege, do the following:

1. Go to www.aftercollege.com and log into your account.

2. On the upper-right menu bar, click My Profile and select View/Edit My Profile.

3. **Scroll all the way to the bottom to the Recommendations section and click Edit.**

The pop-up window shown in Figure 5-4 appears, with all the recommendations you've received, if any.

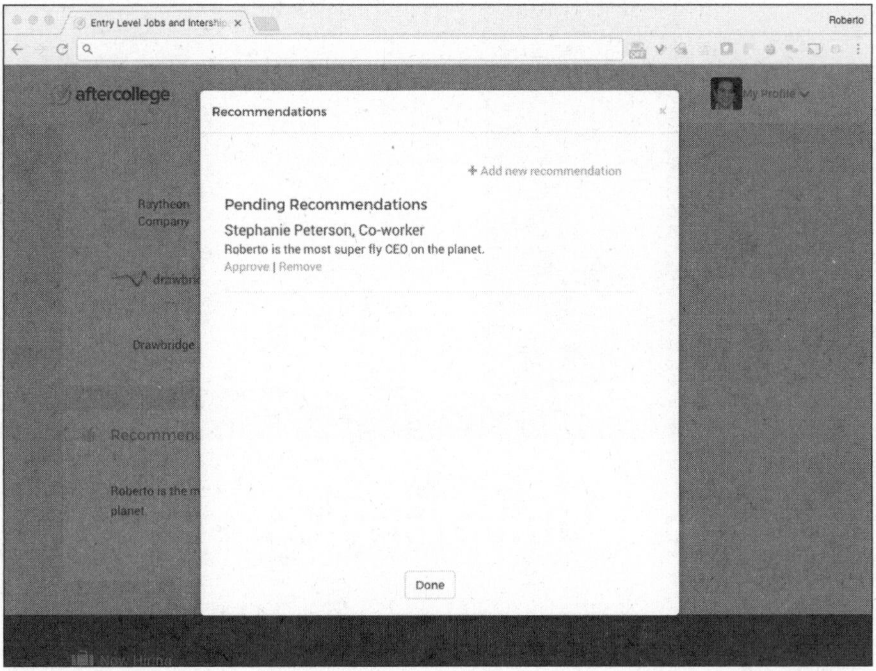

FIGURE 5-4:
Asking for a
recommendation
on AfterCollege.

4. **Click Add New Recommendation.**

5. **Enter the name and email of the person you would like to endorse you.**

You'll see a message template you can use to make your request, as shown in Figure 5-5. You can customize this message as you see fit.

TIP

Add some context to your request, including any specifics that you would like the recommender to mention, such as class projects, skill sets, or knowledge you possess, or a specific accomplishment.

TIP

Use AfterCollege to ask classmates or team members to endorse you. LinkedIn is the most widely used service, but AfterCollege comes in handy when asking for recommendations from those who don't have a LinkedIn profile.

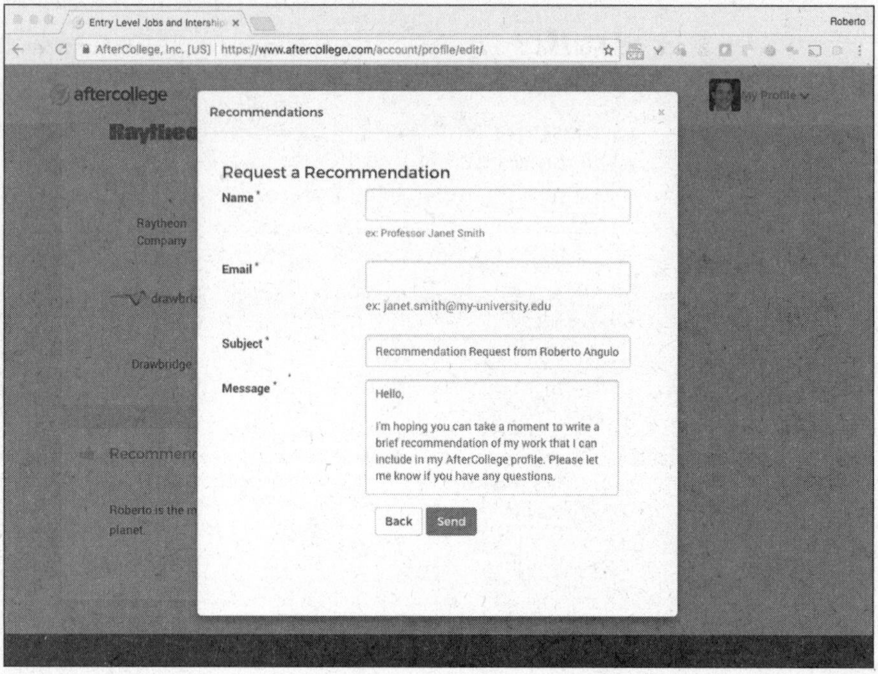

FIGURE 5-5:
Customize the email template as you see fit.

Using Your University Career Center

Your university career center should be one of your first stops as you prepare to look for a job. Career centers are online, allowing you to access them from anywhere, and to easily schedule interviews and sign up for events and workshops.

Good university career centers connect you with alumni and with others outside the organization who can help you find your path. They'll recommend services you can use, whether they're part of the school or not, and they won't pigeonhole you into using only their services. The ecosystem of resources and sites available to you is huge, and effective career centers know this. They do their research and recommend best-of-breed tools for you instead of trying to do everything themselves.

Career centers also organize job fairs and on-campus interviews, which students find effective.

Colleges and universities may have one main career center, a career center for each department or school, or both. Make sure you sign up for every career center you're eligible to use.

Attending career fairs

Among all the services offered by career centers, students rate job and career fairs as the most effective. Career fairs give you an opportunity to meet with a large number of employers in one place, usually walking distance from your classes or dorm room. It doesn't get more convenient than this.

If you're just starting to look for work, make it a point to take an hour or two out of your day to attend an on-campus job fair. These events are usually publicized in the school newspaper or on your career center's website.

Here are some things to remember when attending career fairs:

>> **Do research.** Look at the list of employers attending the career fair and research the ones that interest you by going to their websites.

>> **Show interest.** Sometimes, career centers may have a way for you to express interest in employers prior to the fair. Take advantage of this. The employer may even reach out to you prior to the career fair.

>> **Bring copies of you résumé.** That way, you can drop them off at tables with employers that interest you. You can apply to jobs later, but it doesn't hurt to bring your résumé if you have one.

>> **Take notes.** Take notes after you talk to an employer. You'll want to write down deadlines of when you need to sign up for campus interviews, where to go online to apply for specific positions, and anything else noteworthy that can help you apply later on.

>> **Go early.** Some of the top-brand employers like Google and Tesla will have long lines of students waiting to talk to the recruiters. If you want to avoid waiting in line, go during lunch when all the other students are eating or early while the employers are setting up for the fair.

>> **Connect on LinkedIn.** Connect with recruiters you meet at the fair via LinkedIn if you find out their names.

>> **Learn about new organizations.** Don't limit yourself to organizations you've heard about. Stop by the booths of employers you haven't heard of. You never know! One of them may have your dream job waiting for you.

>> **Don't worry about being perfect.** If you tend to get nervous at interviews or at these types of events, don't worry. It's likely the recruiter won't remember you and you'll most likely interview with a different person once you apply.

>> **Ask about the dress code beforehand.** In general, you don't need to dress formally when you attend job fairs. Most schools allow students to come wearing whatever they wear to class, even if that means jeans or shorts.

Career fairs are generally seen an opportunity for students to do research and for employers to market themselves to students. Employers should be the ones on the spot, not students. That said, some schools do turn away students at the door if they aren't dressed "appropriately." To be safe, make sure to ask about the dress code and follow those guidelines.

TIP

Take advantage of career fairs to learn about new organizations. Go with a group of friends and divide the companies you talk to in order to save time. Then compare notes and share your findings.

Signing up for on-campus interviews

On-campus interviews are usually held shortly after career fairs are held. This is when employers interested in hiring students from your school send representatives to campus. The benefit of these interviews is that they happen on campus and in one convenient location.

Don't delay checking into on-campus interview dates because they vary by industry. For example, the big accounting and consulting firms tend to be on campus very early, as soon as school starts in the fall. On the other hand, government agencies, nonprofits, and firms in other sectors tend to interview later in the school year.

The downside is that not every employer can come to campus. It usually tends to be local employers or large employers that can afford to come to campus.

Sign up for interviews when you're ready. These interviews are the real deal, and you should do your research and prepare before you do an interview.

TIP

Read Chapters 10 and 11 to get more familiar with the interview process and how to prepare.

Practicing with mock interviews

Mock interviews allow you to practice before you do real interviews. Most career centers organize mock interviews by enlisting employers to volunteer to interview on campus and give feedback to students. For employers, it's a chance to build their brand on campus and to identify potential candidates of interest. For you, it's a chance to practice and make a good early impression with prospective employers.

Here are some things you can do to maximize your mock interviews:

>> **Pick a lesser-known employer.** These are practice interviews and employers realize that you're still preparing. Still, if you're worried about making a first impression, start practicing with employers where you're not worried about making the best impression.

>> **Learn from feedback.** Mock interviews are valuable because of the feedback you receive. Write it down or memorize it. But make sure you take any advice you're given and use it to improve your interviewing skills.

>> **Take it easy but take it seriously.** Again, these are practice interviews so don't stress about them. But if you have time, do your research on the interviewer and his organization. You'll need to do research for the real interviews, so you might as well get used to doing this now, even for practice interviews.

>> **Get the interviewer's contact information.** Even if these are practice interviews, you may end up interviewing with the person for real at some point. Take her contact information and send her a thank-you message afterward.

Utilizing other resources on campus

Visit your career center and ask about the resources it has. For example, some career centers offer workshops on writing your résumé and cover letter. You may even be able to get a one-on-one session with a counselor to go over your résumé and to get ideas of things you can do to prepare for your job search.

Some career centers take walk-ins, while others require that you make a reservation to come in. Either way, do this early in the academic year to give yourself plenty of time to prepare and to avoid the last-minute crowds of fellow students.

TIP

Visit your career center's website to find out how you can sign up to receive updates on upcoming events and workshops and follow it on social media.

Deciding to Use Headhunters and Staffing Firms

The topic of using staffing firms and headhunters to help you find a job is a controversial one. To clarify, I'm referring to recruiters who help place you at an organization. I'm not referring to recruiters hired by employers to help them find talent — those folks are hired by the employer and you should view them as being an extension of the employer. I'm talking about people who earn fees on the placements they make. This is where I would exercise caution.

Some people say to use every resource at your disposal to find a job, and in turn, to use a third-party recruiter if it makes it easier for you to find work. I would argue that no one is better qualified to help you find a job you like than you are.

Recruiters are experts in the job placement business. But, at the risk of sounding cheesy, you're the expert in yourself, and this is more important. When you arm yourself with some of the tactics and best practices to find a job, you don't need to hire a staffing firm.

If you do consider working with a staffing firm or headhunter, consider the following:

>> **Who pays?** Do you need to pay a fee or part of your salary to the recruiter if she places you in a job? You shouldn't have to. Even if the employer pays the fee, make sure the recruiter is looking out for your best interests and not placing you at an organization that is paying her the highest finder's fee.

>> **Whose interest do they represent?** Will you get placed at the employer that is the best fit for *you,* or will you get placed in one of a handful of employers with which the staffing firm works? Make sure you know this beforehand.

>> **Is there time pressure?** Can you take your time in deciding where to work or do you have to make a decision within a certain time frame?

>> **What impression will you make?** Some employers don't mind whether you apply via a third-party recruiter or if you apply directly. Others may. Some employers will state on their sites that they don't take applications from third-party recruiters.

These are some of the questions you should ask before enlisting the help of a third-party recruiter to help you find a job.

Chapter **6**

Searching for Jobs Online

J ob sites make it easy for you to search for work. Just type in your desired keywords and you'll get a list back with matching jobs. Some of the better sites offer filters on the side so you can narrow your results.

In this chapter, you learn some tricks to help you get an edge over other job seekers. Even if you're not technical, you can use some simple search techniques such as Boolean operators to uncover the right job listings. For example, you may want to include management trainee jobs in your search, but exclude those that are in food service or retail. Boolean lets you do this. In another case, you may want to look for jobs that include *copywriting, content marketing,* or *journalism* in the description. You can run three separate searches or just do one using Boolean operators.

When you know about these techniques, you can use them not just on job sites, but also on search engines like Google, allowing you to uncover opportunities that may not be obvious.

Finally, you gain knowledge of how to set up search notifications that will email you new jobs as they become available.

Familiarizing Yourself with Search Techniques

Don't let the title of this section fool you. You don't need to learn sophisticated search mechanics to do an effective job search. Most job sites are designed to let even novice job seekers access relevant jobs. But knowing some simple search tactics (which may sound complicated, but really aren't), you can speed up your search and uncover entry-level jobs and internships more easily.

Conducting a basic job search

Popular job sites, like Indeed, give you a keyword field and a location box to start your search, as shown in Figure 6-1. Usually this is all you need. Type in a keyword or two and an optional location to start your query.

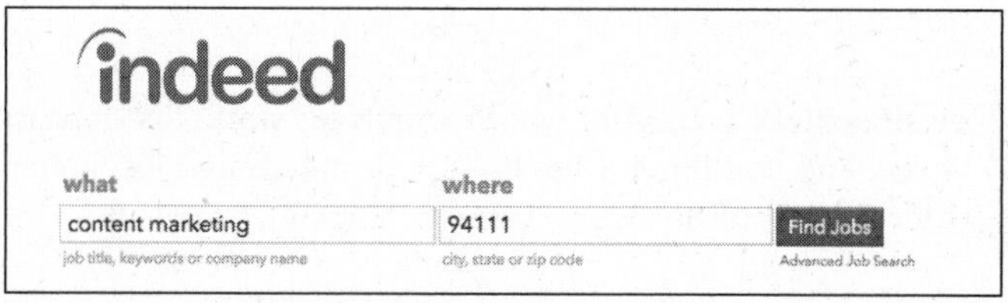

FIGURE 6-1:
Doing a basic keyword and location search on Indeed.

TIP

In the location field, try your search with a zip code first and then try it again with a city-and-state combination. Because jobs are classified differently, one search may show you more jobs than the other.

Your results will most likely contain filters that you can use to narrow your search by location, type of job, and even employer, as shown in Figure 6-2. These filters may seem obvious, but they're powerful because they guide you into knowing what kind of jobs exists in your area of interest and where they're located. You can click in and out of these filtered lists to get a good idea of the opportunities available to you.

TIP

Are you willing to work anywhere for the right job? Leave the location field blank and search only by keyword. This will yield more results and give you ideas of jobs to pursue. You can take a deeper dive by using the filters provided.

Job sites vary in functionality. Some offer filters where you can narrow your results after you've done a keyword search. Others, like Craigslist, start you out with a navigation menu where you first select a city, then a job category, and drill down from there. But what all these sites have in common is that they provide a keyword search field somewhere in the search, either at the start or as you narrow your results.

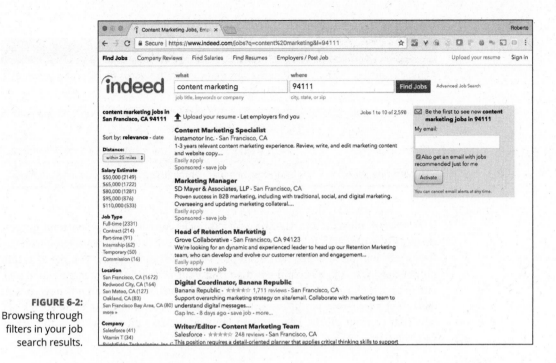

FIGURE 6-2:
Browsing through filters in your job search results.

Using keywords

You'll probably use more than one keyword in your job search. For example, you may search for some of these jobs: marketing analyst, financial analyst, or summer internship.

The results you get will vary based on how you enter these search terms. On most sites, if you enter **financial analyst**, you will get more results than when you enter **"financial analyst"** (with double quotes).

The double quotes tell the job site to treat your search as an exact phrase, meaning, the site searches for the exact term *financial analyst* in the job title or job description, as opposed to searching for both words — *financial* and *analyst* — in any order anywhere in the job listing. Table 6-1 shows these and other variations.

TIP

Some sites interpret the use of double quotes as intent to search for an exact term. Other sites ignore double quotes, and some sites block quotes altogether. The takeaway here is to try your search both ways — with quotes and without quotes — and adjust when you see the results you like.

TABLE 6-1

Varying Your Keyword Job Searches

Keyword Combination	Resulting Search
financial analyst	Returns jobs that contain the words *financial* and *analyst* in any order.
analyst financial	Returns jobs that contain the words *financial* and *analyst* in any order.
"financial analyst"	Returns jobs that contain the exact phrase *financial analyst*.
"analyst financial"	Returns jobs that contain the exact phrase *analyst financial*.

Narrow your job search further by using three keywords or more, without quotes. On sites like Indeed, LinkedIn, and AfterCollege, the more keywords you use, the fewer jobs will be returned. For example, search for *content,* and you get a certain number of jobs. Add a second word so that your search is now *content marketing,* and your search returns fewer jobs. Add a third word, so your search is now *content marketing intern,* and you'll see even fewer jobs. This is because sites search for jobs that contain all the keywords in your query. Use more keywords to narrow your search.

TIP

Job sites handle keyword searches differently. For example, CareerBuilder.com, unlike Indeed, will show you more jobs as you enter more keywords. Try your search on each site you use and compare the results on each to see how they differ.

Performing Boolean searches

Another good way to hone your search is to use Boolean operators. Don't worry, it's a fancy name, but the concept is simple. Boolean is a way for you to do searches using AND, OR, and NOT operators. These operators come in handy because they allow you to do searches that include some words but exclude others.

For example, you can search for entry-level jobs that are economics related, but are not in sales, using the following query:

"entry-level" OR internship AND economics NOT sales

Because the term *entry-level* contains a hyphen, you may need to put it in double quotes.

I used this search string on Indeed, and it worked pretty well, as you can see in Figure 6-3. It tells the site to find jobs that contain either the term *entry-level* or the word *internship* anywhere in the posting. I use these because they tend to be included in most jobs that require no experience. You could also include the term *"no experience"* (with quotes) to expand your results. I then add *AND economics* to specify that the job must contain the word *economics.* Finally, because I don't want to include listings having to do with sales, I add *NOT sales* in the query string.

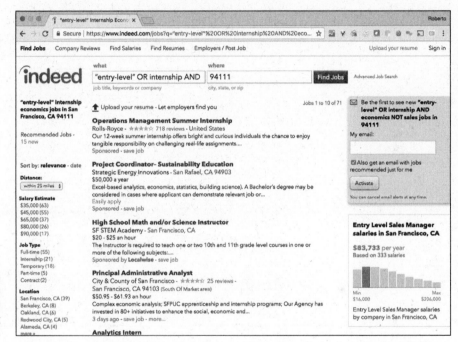

FIGURE 6-3:
Boolean search and corresponding results on Indeed.

REMEMBER

When using the NOT operator for a specific word, your search will exclude any jobs with that word, whether or not it pertains to the job. For example, if you use *NOT sales,* any job with the word *sales* will be removed, even if *sales* applies to the company description and not to the job itself.

You can take advantage of other operators in addition to the ones in this example. Table 6-2 gives you a quick guide of Boolean terms you can use in your searches.

With practice and some trial and error, you will master Boolean operators so you can make the most out of searching for jobs.

TABLE 6-2

Useful Boolean Operators to Use in Your Job Search

Operator	Description
AND	Use AND to include all the keywords in your search. For example, *project AND coordinator* returns jobs that include both words. Some sites automatically assume you want all words included and don't require you to use AND. On other sites you do need to use AND.
+	This is the same as AND. Some sites use +, while others use AND.
OR	Use OR to find jobs that include any one of your keywords. For example, *project OR coordinator* returns jobs that include at least one of the keywords but not necessarily both.
NOT	Use NOT to exclude jobs that include a certain keyword. For example, searching with *NOT director* excludes jobs that include the word *director* in them.
–	This is the same as NOT. Some sites use –, while others use NOT.
" "	Use double quotes to ensure the site searches for the specific term you enter. This is useful when a term has two or more words or special characters such as a dash. For example, searching for *"entry-level"* returns jobs that contain this exact term.
( )	Use parentheses to make your search easier to read and to ensure your search performs as you want it to work. For example, use *(sales OR marketing OR finance) AND (internship OR "entry-level" OR beginner)* to find jobs that contain at least one of the keywords in the first set AND also at least one of the keywords in the second set.
*	Use the wildcard asterisk to find variations of a word. For example, searching for *intern** will return jobs containing the words *intern, interns, internship,* and *internships.* Be careful, though, as it will also return jobs containing words like *internal, international,* and so on.

Doing an advanced job search

If doing Boolean job searches is too much for you, don't worry. Some sites, like Indeed, give you the option to do advanced job searches that take care of the logic for you behind the scenes. Figure 6-4 illustrates what one of these search screens looks like.

The advanced search lets you specify the words you want to include in all the search results, as well as the words you want to exclude. In Indeed's case, you can also specify the type of job, you can restrict your keywords to the title only, and you can search for specific employers.

Each job site is different and offers additional search functionality based on the data it collects from employers.

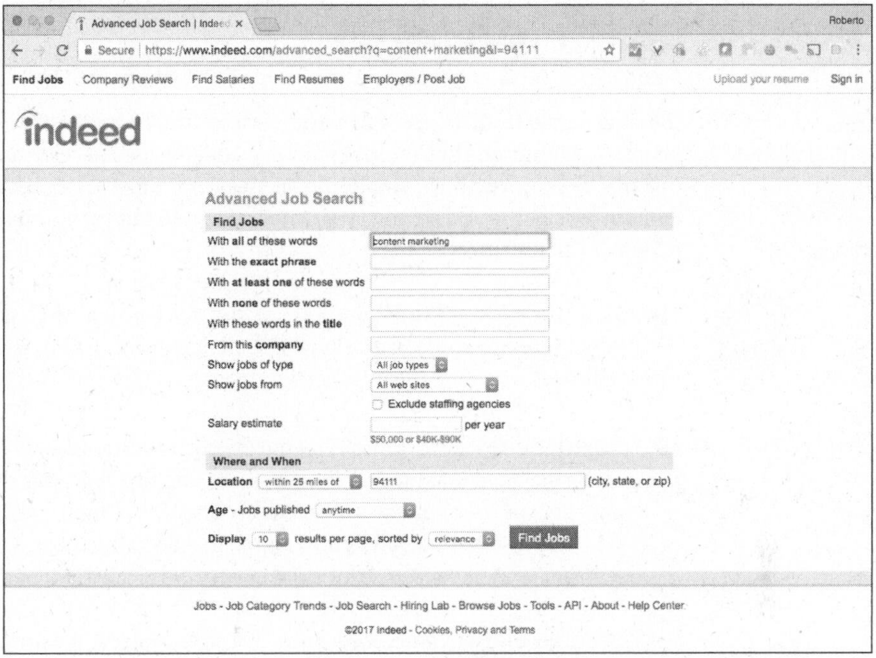

FIGURE 6-4: Boolean search and corresponding results on Indeed.

SIGNING UP FOR JOB ALERTS AND UPDATES FOR A SPECIFIC EMPLOYER

TECHNICAL STUFF

If you're really interested in a specific employer, go to its website and find the careers section. Most medium to large employers have one. You can sign up for job alerts from the employer and get event updates. You'll need to enter your email address or create an account. For example, Disney has a careers section at http://jobs.disneycareers.com where you can register for updates. You don't need to have your résumé ready, and you don't need to apply to any jobs if you're not ready. But you gain two advantages by going to the employer's site:

- **You get the inside scoop.** You stay informed about new jobs as soon as they're posted.

- **Get on the employer's radar.** A recruiter may see that you've signed up on the company's site and reach out to you to start the recruiting process.

Searching on Job Sites

Job sites come in different sizes and vary in functionality. The large national job boards list hundreds of thousands of jobs and give you access to these jobs through one place. Then you have smaller local sites that have fewer listings, but they may contain jobs not found on the large sites. (For a list of recommended job sites, take a look at Chapter 16.)

TIP

Most first-time job seekers complain about not being able to find enough entry-level jobs. Here are some of the types of sites you can use to find your first job or internship:

>> **Large job sites:** Sites in this category include Monster (www.monster.com), CareerBuilder (www.careerbuilder.com), and top aggregator Indeed (www.indeed.com). These sites contain hundreds of thousands of opportunities. They also tend to offer good search functionality, support for Boolean searches, and filters. Quantity is not always the answer, though. Just because a site has a lot of jobs that doesn't mean it has the right jobs for you and especially the right entry-level ones. Still, take a look at these sites.

>> **Local regional sites:** Craigslist is a good example here. While it's a large site with international reach, Craigslist (www.craigslist.org) is organized into regional sites, giving you good visibility into local employers. Newspaper sites also offer great local jobs. Sites like http://jobs.bnd.com in Belleville, Illinois, and www.jobsok.com in Oklahoma offer hyper-targeted access to local employers.

>> **Audience-specific sites:** If you're a college student or recent grad, sites like AfterCollege (www.aftercollege.com) and College Recruiter (www.collegerecruiter.com) give you access to jobs and internships from employers looking specifically for entry-level candidates.

>> **Industry-specific sites:** Dice (www.dice.com) and Health eCareers (www.healthecareers.com) are two examples of sites that cater to those interested in the technology and healthcare sectors, respectively.

>> **Association sites:** Are you focused on a specific field of study? If so, sites like the IEEE Job Site (http://careers.ieee.org) and the American Accounting Association Career Center (http://careercenter.aaahq.org) allow you to search for jobs that are targeted to your field of study.

TIP

Check with any group of which you're a member to see if it has its own job site.

Finding Jobs on Google

Google is a great place to search for anything, including jobs. Although it's not a job site per se, Google crawls content from all over the Internet, including job content from employer websites. It indexes jobs from various job sites.

The other great thing about Google is that it allows you to use Boolean operators. If you like Boolean, you can use it on Google to do searches to your heart's content.

You can enter the same search string from "Performing Boolean searches," earlier in this chapter, into Google to search for jobs. Google will return relevant search results, including jobs. Click the jobs section in the results and you'll be taken to a section on Google that lets you do job searches, as shown in Figure 6-5.

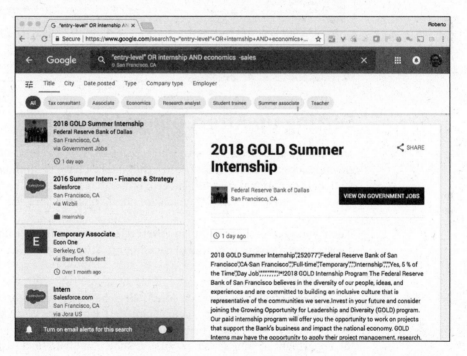

FIGURE 6-5: Searching for jobs on Google.

As you search for jobs on Google, it will recognize these searches and customize the results page for you, giving you filters so you can drill down by location, job title, type of job, company type, and employer.

TIP

You may be tempted to skip the job sites all together and just use Google. But Google doesn't index all job content, so you should still use job sites.

Setting Up Automatic Job Alerts

Most sites, including Google, allow you to set up email job alerts. This way, you can get notified of new jobs coming out that match your search criteria. Take advantage of these automatic notifications, because they save you time. They also give you a head start so you can apply to any job of interest as soon as the job is discovered.

Google, for example, gives you the option of setting up a job alert for any search you do. Just activate the job alert setting in the lower-left corner of your browser when doing a job search. Figure 6-6 illustrates how easy it is to activate these alerts.

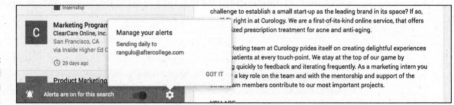

FIGURE 6-6: Activating email job alerts on Google.

Setting up AfterCollege job alerts

AfterCollege is focused exclusively on helping college students and recent graduates find jobs and internships. Although it doesn't have the number of jobs found on Google or national sites like Indeed, it does have a large number of entry-level jobs and internships, some of which are not found anywhere else.

When you create an account on AfterCollege, you automatically get daily job digests based on your educational background. After a few weeks, these digests go from daily to weekly.

You can also create job alerts on AfterCollege based on your searches. To do this, go to www.aftercollege.com/search and do a job search. When you're comfortable with the results, click the Notify Me When Similar Jobs Are Posted button on the upper right of your search results, as shown in Figure 6-7.

Follow individual employers and get notified when they post new jobs. When you're on a job listing, click Follow This Company in the upper-right corner of the posting, as shown in Figure 6-8.

You can always unsubscribe from job alerts and stop getting employer notifications by logging on to AfterCollege and updating your communications settings.

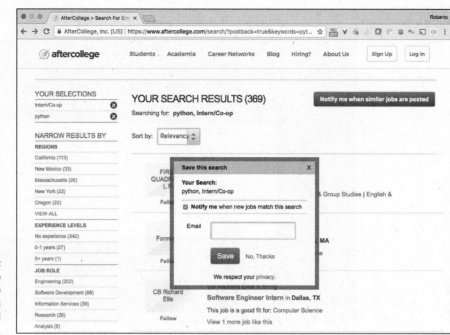

FIGURE 6-7:
Setting up AfterCollege job alerts based on your entry-level job search.

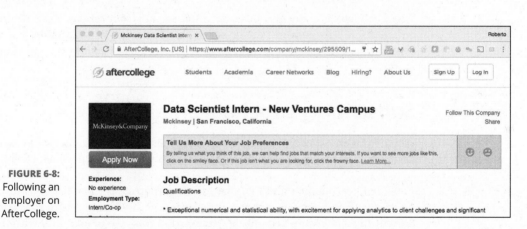

FIGURE 6-8:
Following an employer on AfterCollege.

Creating a LinkedIn job notification

LinkedIn is known for being the top professional network, but it also holds its own against sites like Indeed and has hundreds of thousands of jobs, including entry-level ones. Create a LinkedIn job alert by going to www.linkedin.com/jobs and doing a search. Click Create Search Alert on the right of the search results, as shown in Figure 6-9. You can choose to get your alerts via email, via the LinkedIn app, via LinkedIn.com, or from all three.

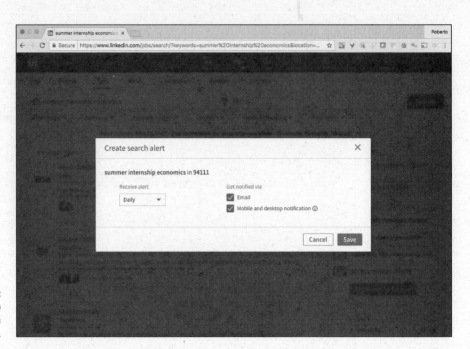

FIGURE 6-9:
Creating a job search alert on LinkedIn.

When you look at a job on LinkedIn, you'll see any connections you have to the organization. The convenience of being able to see a job description and your connections at the same time makes LinkedIn a valuable tool to have in your job search.

Subscribing to school email lists

When I was in college, I remember getting most of my best internship and job leads from my academic department and from student groups to which I belonged.

I majored in economics and I was part of the department email list. As a result, I heard about not-so-publicized recruiting events with companies such as McKinsey & Company and Boston Consulting Group, and I was able to interview with them. Often, employers miss campus recruiting deadlines and go directly to academic departments to see if they can interview students.

Toward the end of my junior year, I started becoming interested in industrial engineering and started taking classes. I subscribed to the department's email distribution list, which was managed by the department administrator. Through this list, I became aware of a summer internship at a company called Intuit. It wanted an intern to build a website for a new initiative. I only knew a little about web development, but because it was late in the summer and Intuit needed someone, I got the internship. This was the best internship ever! I learned a lot and the experience got me exposed to the world of technology. My boss at the time, Ravi, put his faith in my ability to do what needed to get done, and he gave me a chance. All this because of a lead I got via the industrial engineering email list!

I also belonged to the Mexican Student Association, as I had come from Mexico, and I was on the member email list. In one instance, I got a message about the Mexican minister of finance visiting campus and offering to meet with ten students who were interested in working in Mexico. I was one of the first students to reply. As a result, I ended up having coffee with the finance minister, who offered to make introductions for me.

TIP

If you belong to any student groups, subscribe to their distribution lists. Do the same with your academic department. These are valuable affiliations that can generate great job leads for you.

Using IFTTT notifications and Craigslist

Craigslist is a massive classifieds site, with a lot of local jobs listed. The site is simple and easy to use, but it doesn't offer a way to get email alerts when new jobs are posted. Luckily, a site called IFTTT lets you create email notifications for other sites, including Craigslist. So when a new job gets posted that is relevant to you, you receive an alert.

To set up an IFTTT alert based on a Craigslist search, do the following:

1. Go to www.craigslist.org.

    The site will redirect to the local version of Craigslist for your city.

2. Navigate to the Jobs section and drill down to find the types of jobs you like.

3. When you see the results you like, copy the URL from your browser, as shown in Figure 6-10.

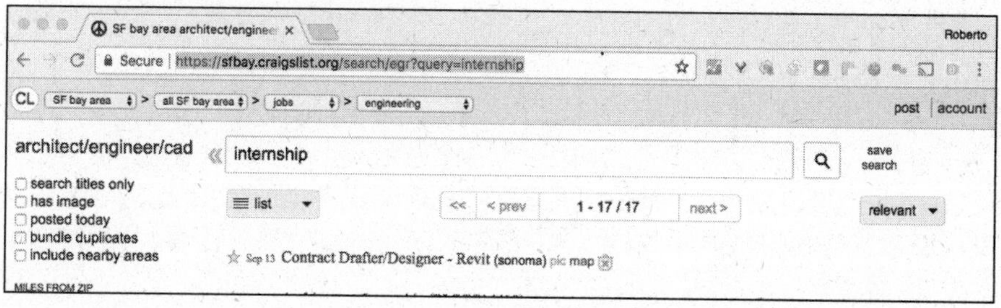

FIGURE 6-10:
Getting the URL for your job search results on Craigslist.

4. Go to www.ifttt.com and either create an account or log in.

5. Go to www.ifttt.com/search and search for Craigslist.

6. Select the first result that says Get an Email Whenever a New Craigslist Post Matches Your Search, as shown in Figure 6-11.

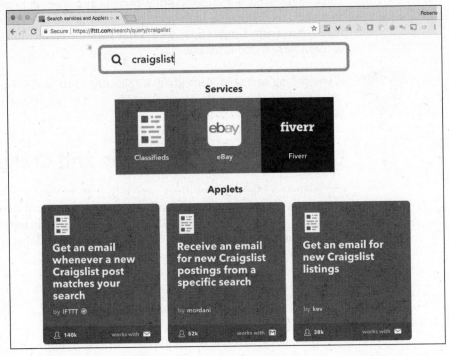

FIGURE 6-11:
Setting up
Craigslist on
IFTTT.

You'll see the applet page.

7. Turn on the switch that says Receive Notifications When This Applet Runs, and below that, enter the Craigslist search URL you copied in Step 3, as shown in Figure 6-12.

FIGURE 6-12:
Activating your
Craigslist
notification
on IFTTT.

8. **Click Save.**

You can discontinue your IFTTT notifications and edit them at any time.

Chapter 7

Building a Great Online Presence

Almost nothing on the Internet is private. If people want to find out about you, all they have to do is go to Google and type in your name. Count on most employers doing this when considering you for a job. Many will even look you up on social media to see if you have profiles and to look at what you post.

This chapter shows you how to be proactive and have more control over what employers see about you online. You learn to create job seeker profiles so recruiters can find you more easily. You also get guidance on how to showcase your work online. Social media and blogs give you a great platform through which you can share insights and knowledge. If you're knowledgeable in world affairs, share your opinions and reasoning with others. Do you know about web hosting platforms and the various options available to people wanting to build a website? You can write about this and help others while also impressing your future employer. Did you take a class on how to build financial models to evaluate projects? Share your knowledge via a blog post.

This is also the time to take inventory of what you post and share online. Look at your Twitter, Instagram, and Facebook accounts for any questionable pictures. Were you tagged in a photo while riding a skateboard and smoking from a bong? Although that's an impressive feat, you're better off being safe than sorry and untagging yourself in that picture.

Creating a LinkedIn Profile

Having a LinkedIn profile is almost as important as having a résumé. If you have one, employers will find you more easily when searching for you online. More important, they'll get a first impression of you based on what's in your profile. Use this to your advantage by creating a good profile and making sure you at least have your educational background listed, some skills, and any internship or work experience.

To create a LinkedIn profile:

1. **Go to www.linkedin.com.**

2. **Enter your name, your email address, and a password, and click Join Now.**

   On the next screen, you'll be asked if you're currently a student.

3. **Even if you're a recent graduate, click Yes and enter your school and graduation year.**

   This part is important because it will customize what you see based on your school.

   When you click to the next step, you'll be asked what you're interested in.

4. **Choose Finding a Job.**

   The next steps will ask you to import your contacts or connect to people from your school or from your city.

5. **You can skip these steps or choose to connect with people you recognize.**

   Eventually, you'll be taken to your profile, where you can continue adding content to your profile.

Initially you may find it hard to add to your LinkedIn profile. Here are some essential components you can start with:

>> **Picture:** Add a nice headshot to your profile. Having a profile photo adds a personal touch and makes it easier for people to remember you. Just make sure it looks professional.

>> **Summary:** A summary is similar to your objective on a résumé. You can add something along the lines of "Stanford University economics grad looking to add value as a financial analyst" or "Samuel Merritt nursing student looking to serve patients in a community-based hospital."

>> **Skills:** Add some skills to your profile. This can include any computer software you're proficient in (for example, Microsoft Word, Microsoft Excel, Adobe Photoshop, and so on) or a skill like financial analysis. You should include here anything that you can do well, as shown in Figure 7-1.

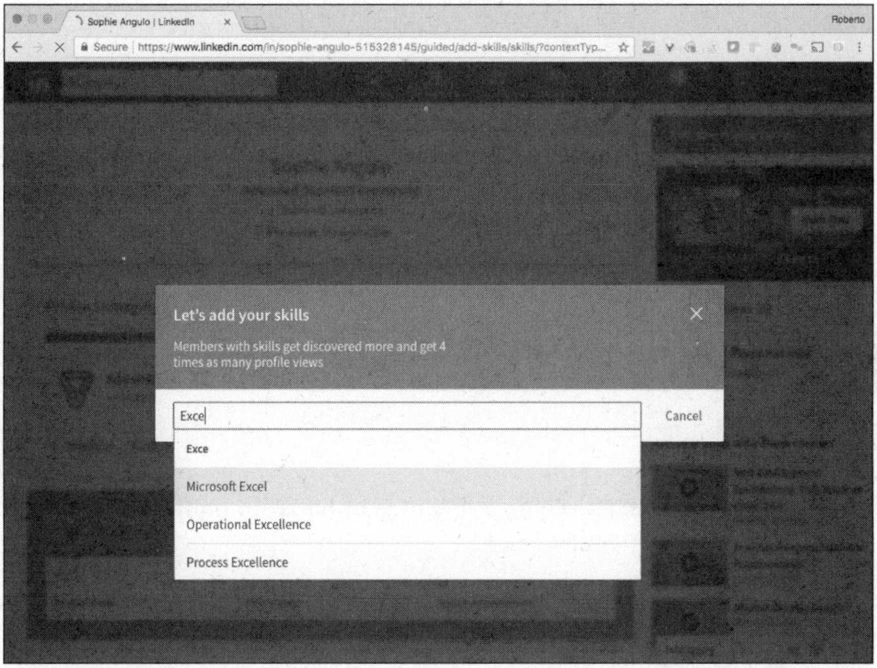

FIGURE 7-1:
Adding skills to your LinkedIn profile.

>> **Experience:** This book is about getting your first job, so you may not have any professional experience. But think of any activities you've done at school, part-time jobs, work-study, or any volunteer work. Those count as experience!

Need ideas on what to add to your LinkedIn profile? Check out the section about detailing your experience in Chapter 2.

TIP

Create a custom URL for your profile. You can do this by clicking the preferences icon at the upper right, under Public Profile Settings. Under Edit Public Profile URL (see Figure 7-2), enter the URL you want. Just make sure it's something straightforward and professional, like your first initial and last name, or your first name and last name separated by a period (or not separated at all).

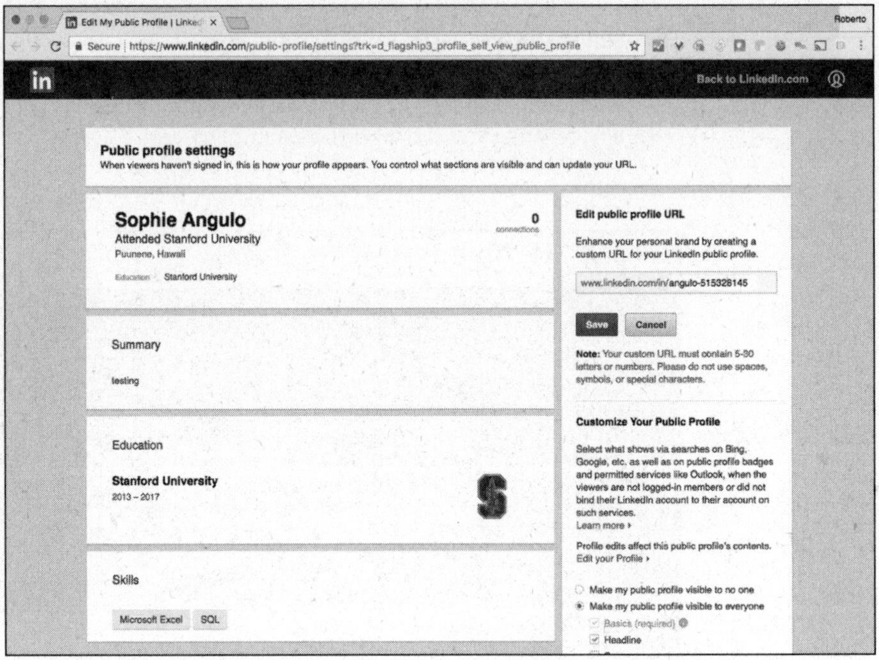

FIGURE 7-2:
Customizing your public profile URL on LinkedIn.

TIP

Consider adding a link to your LinkedIn profile on your résumé, under contact information.

REMEMBER

Your LinkedIn profile is an ongoing work in progress. Every time you add work experience, acquire a skill, or create a new body of work, make sure to update your profile.

Setting Up an AfterCollege Student Profile

Create an AfterCollege profile if you're a college student or a recent graduate. Similar to a LinkedIn profile, it allows you to showcase your work. But unlike LinkedIn, which is used mainly by employers looking to find experienced talent, AfterCollege is used by employers specifically looking for entry-level candidates like you. As a result, when you create an AfterCollege profile, you increase your chances of being contacted by an employer.

Jenea is a recent graduate who graduated cum laude with a BS degree in applied mathematics from the University of Pittsburgh. She created an AfterCollege profile soon after graduation and started following companies. One of these was the Bank of New York Mellon. Staffers saw her profile on AfterCollege and hired her.

Follow these steps to create a profile on AfterCollege:

1. **Go to www.aftercollege.com.**

2. **Click Sign Up at the upper right of the screen.**

3. **Enter your name, your email address, and a password, and click Let's Get Started.**

4. **Upload a résumé if you have one and click Next.**

   AfterCollege will automatically read your résumé and use it to pre-populate fields in the forms to follow.

5. **Enter your school, major, graduation date, and location, and click Next.**

   If you uploaded a résumé, you'll notice these fields are already filled in.

   After you enter information about your education, you'll be taken to your profile page.

6. Edit your profile, as shown in Figure 7-3.

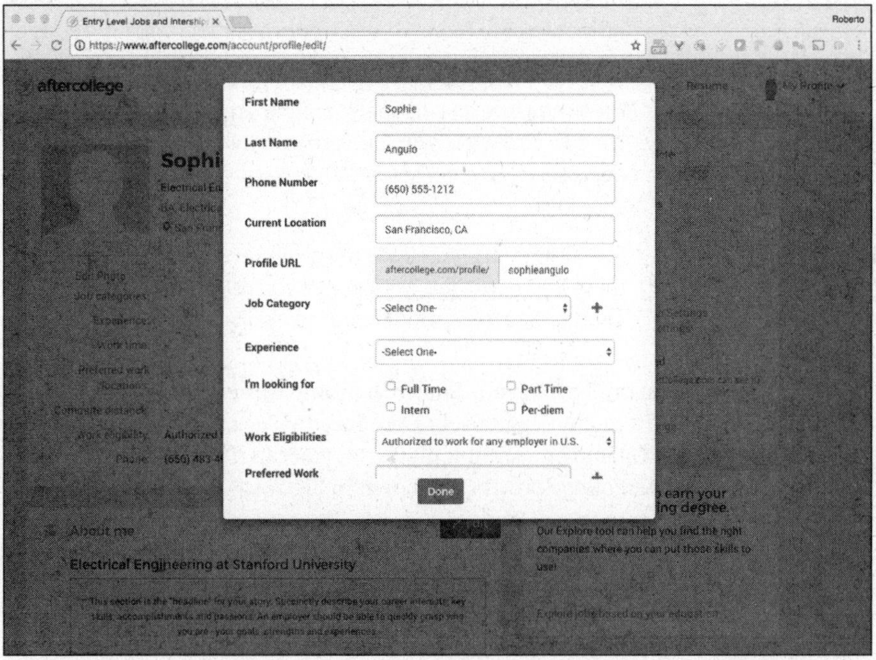

FIGURE 7-3: Editing your AfterCollege profile.

TIP

School, major, and grad year are the most important fields in your AfterCollege profile because they're what employers use to find you.

One thing you'll notice about your profile is that you don't need to enter a lot of information in order to fill it out. AfterCollege profiles are designed for college students, who don't have a lot of experience under their belts.

These are the key pieces of information you need to fill out in addition to adding your school, major, and graduation date:

>> **Picture:** Similar to your LinkedIn profile, adding a picture to your AfterCollege profile allows you to stand out. It also makes it easier for people to remember you.

>> **Accomplishments:** Employers like to see extracurricular activities and accomplishments. Scholarship awards are a good example of these. Were you part of a sports team? Enter this information here, especially if you won any competitions. You can also mention being a member of an honor society, fraternity, or sorority. If you held an executive role in one of these groups, enter this as part of your experience.

>> **Preferred work locations:** You can add as many as you want. This also allows AfterCollege to target the right jobs based on your locations of interest.

>> **Skills and languages (see Figure 7-4):** Enter as many skills as you want. If you speak any foreign languages, enter them here along with your level of fluency. You can also enter skills and programming languages. You also have an opportunity to enter *soft skills* (personal attributes that can help you in doing your job).

TIP

Soft skills or attributes are not always easy to identify. Employers look for these in order to gauge how well you will do in a specific role. Check out Chapter 2 to learn more about soft skills.

You can link to your LinkedIn profile from AfterCollege. More important, if you've written any blog posts or produced videos, or if you have a code repository stored on GitHub or a similar platform, you can link to all these bodies of work from your AfterCollege profile, as shown in Figure 7-5.

Your college or university may have an e-portfolio system to help you keep track of projects or papers you've written. If they do, then leverage this resource and include a link to your e-portfolio on your AfterCollege profile.

TIP

You may find yourself struggling to figure out what to include in your profile. But remember, you've written papers, and these are worth including.

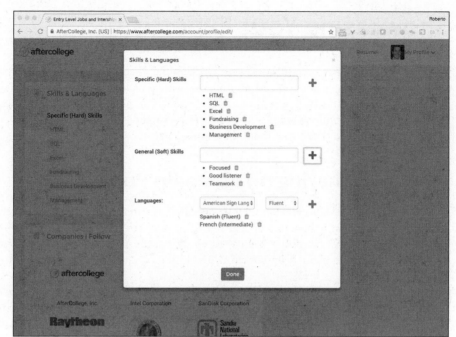

FIGURE 7-4:
Entering skills and languages on AfterCollege.

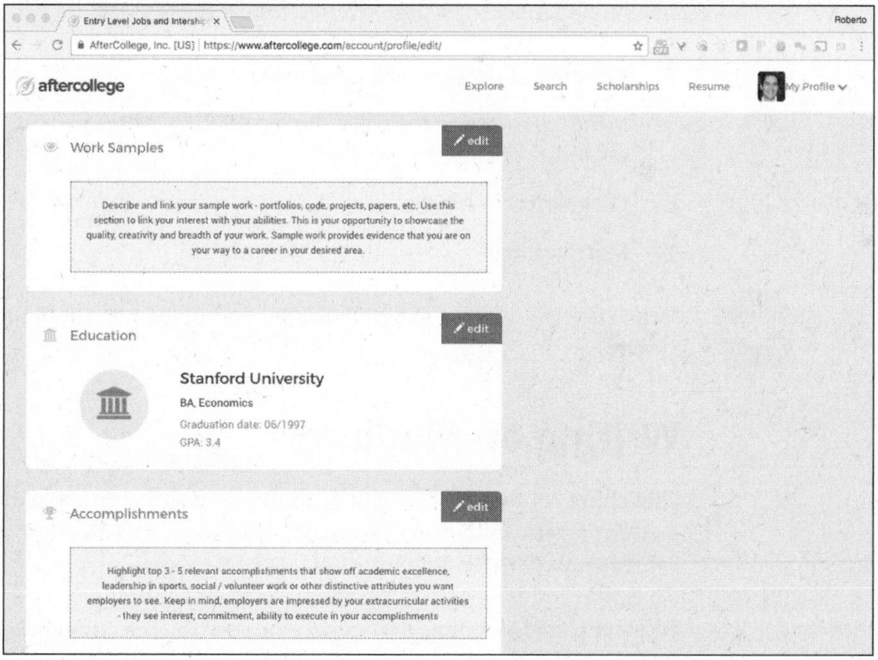

FIGURE 7-5:
Linking to other profiles and work from your AfterCollege profile.

Showcasing Your Expertise

It's easy to show off your work online. If you have a blog, or you've written extensively about a certain topic, or you've posted the results of a class project where you achieved a good outcome, you can share this with prospective employers. Recruiters who look at your résumé and profile will often dig deeper to learn about you if you give them the chance to do so.

Sharing on LinkedIn Publishing

LinkedIn Publishing is a popular platform for posting opinion pieces and anything that is business or marketing centric. For example, I tend to write about entry-level recruiting trends, using data from AfterCollege, to share with my contacts and publicly on LinkedIn.

The advantage to publishing on LinkedIn is that your posts appear automatically in your profile. They're also seen across your network of LinkedIn connections. And unlike other LinkedIn features, you can share your posts with others even if they aren't LinkedIn members.

Posting on LinkedIn is simple if you follow these steps:

1. **Go to www.linkedin.com and log in.**

   In the top middle of the page, you see a section where you can share articles, photos, or updates.

2. **Click Write an Article.**

3. **Start writing!**

TIP

Make sure you write a catchy headline and upload a graphic to accompany your article.

Writing on Medium

Publishing content on Medium is similar to writing on LinkedIn. Both are strong platforms with millions of users. You can log on to Medium using your Google, Facebook, or Twitter account.

To start using Medium, just go to www.medium.com and click Write a Story. It's that simple! When you write on Medium, you'll need to manually add your articles to your LinkedIn and AfterCollege profiles.

Medium is a good platform to use if you have a lot of Twitter followers. These services integrate well with each other, so when you connect your Medium and Twitter accounts, anything you publish on Medium can be easily shared with your Twitter followers.

You can choose between writing on Medium or writing on LinkedIn, or you can post your articles to both.

Creating content on YouTube

Video isn't for everyone, but if you're good in front of a camera, you should consider recording a short video introduction about yourself and posting it on YouTube.

You can record a video using your phone's camera. A simple introduction could be something like the following:

> Hello,
>
> My name is Roberto Angulo, and I'm a recent economics graduate from Stanford University. I'm looking to do great work as a business analyst at a growing company that is making a positive impact on society. I'm very knowledgeable about data analysis and enjoy identifying trends in numbers to help improve business processes and outcomes.
>
> I look forward to talking to you about opportunities at your organization. Thank you for your consideration!

If your work has led you to create other projects that you can showcase via video, make sure to include these in your profiles.

Showing off your code on GitHub

GitHub is a collaboration tool for programmers to share their code and to review other developers' work. It also comes with a profile that allows you to display your programming accomplishments and your contributions to code repositories that you or others create, as you can see in Figure 7-6.

If you're a computer science student, you're most likely using GitHub already to submit assignments. You can create a personalized GitHub URL and include it in your AfterCollege profile.

Learn more about GitHub at www.github.com.

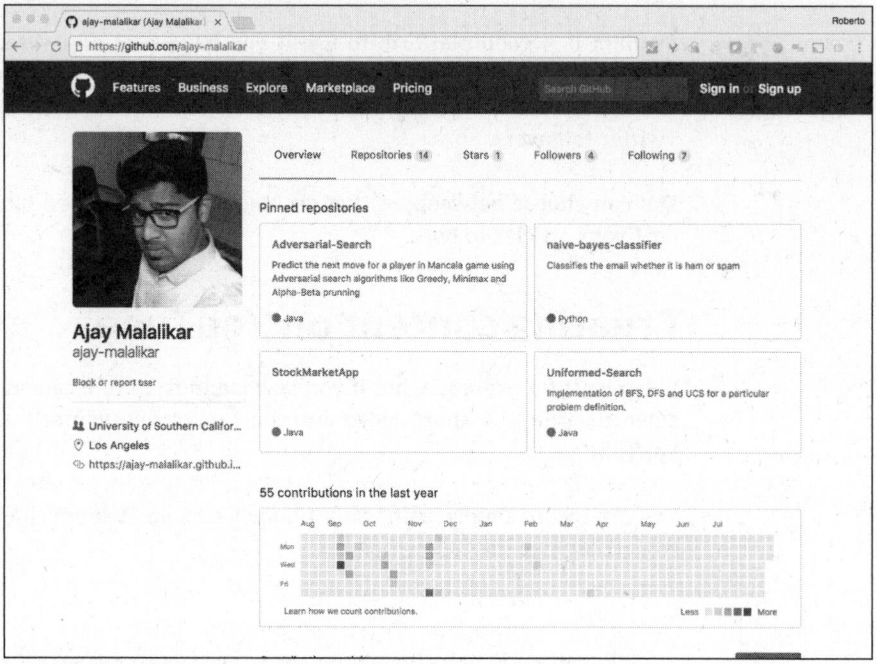

FIGURE 7-6:
Example of a GitHub profile.

Competing on Kaggle

Kaggle is similar to GitHub but it's more of a platform for competitions and it's focused on data science. On Kaggle, you compete as part of a team with other Kaggle members, or on your own, to solve data science challenges. Some of these challenges are posted by employers looking to find talented candidates.

If you're good at solving data problems, consider taking part in competitions. You can show off your rank on Kaggle, as shown in Figure 7-7. And you can customize your Kaggle URL and add a link to your LinkedIn profile from your Kaggle profile.

Learn more about Kaggle at www.kaggle.com.

REMEMBER

Add a link to your Kaggle profile to your LinkedIn and AfterCollege profiles.

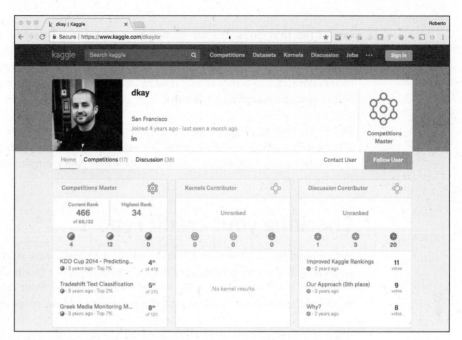

FIGURE 7-7:
Example of a
great Kaggle
profile.

Cleaning Up Your Online Presence

You've put in time and effort to build out your professional profile and to show-case your work. This is a major step and you deserve a pat on the back. But now it's time to take inventory of what you've posted online, or what's been posted about you, and clean up anything that may work against you in your quest for your first job.

Make a list of any social media accounts you have, even old ones you don't use, so you can make sure they're free of any potentially incriminating pictures or posts.

TIP

If you have any social media accounts tied to your school email address, make sure you update them with a new address before you graduate. (Schools often expire student email addresses after they graduate.) This way, if you ever forget any of your social media passwords, you can still do a password lookup.

Searching for yourself on Google

Google is the most widely used search engine so start there. You can get a good idea of what's posted about you online by going to Google and searching for your name. Try searching for your name with and without quotation marks (for exam-ple, *Roberto Angulo* and *"Roberto Angulo"*).

One of the first links you see should be your LinkedIn profile. Make sure your profile is up to date. If you see pages for other people with your same name, there's not much you can do about it. I share my name with a Peruvian senator, a former Mexican governor who's now in jail for corruption, and a great artist who paints realistic watercolor portraits.

Make sure that any pages that relate to you are accurate and free of any compromising information. Google is great because it displays the pages where you need to update your information. These are the same pages employers will see when they look you up.

Checking your credit report

You're looking for your first job and you're most likely just starting to establish your credit history by getting a credit card and being more financially independent. Employers often do credit checks on new potential hires. Your credit score serves as an indication of how well you handle finances and how responsible you are.

Although employers may not run a credit check on you for your first job, they may run credit checks for future jobs. So, it's important that you keep a clean credit history. You can get a free copy of your credit report by going to www.annualcreditreport.com.

You have a right to one free copy of your report every 12 months from each of the three nationwide credit reporting companies. You'll need to provide your name, address, Social Security number, and birth date in order to get your report.

Dealing with a DUI or arrest record

If you've ever been arrested for driving under the influence (DUI) or for another offense, this information may appear online. Unfortunately, this can hurt your chances of getting a job if employers see it online or find it in a background check.

Depending on the state where you live, you may be able to have your record sealed or expunged, and in this way, prevent the information from appearing online or in a background check. Some states are so strict that your record can only be expunged via a pardon from the governor. Other states make it easier if you're a juvenile or if it's your first offense. DUIs tend to result in two records — a driving or DMV record and a criminal record. To get your records sealed or expunged, you'll need to contact the DMV and your state's attorney general's office. Your best bet is to hire a DUI attorney to look into this for you. It'll cost you money, but it may be worth it.

TIP

If you're sure your DUI record won't appear online or in a background check anymore because it's been sealed or expunged, you may be able to get away with not telling a prospective employer about your DUI. This depends on how the question is being asked. If an employer asks you if you've been convicted of a crime, and you were arrested for a DUI but not convicted, then you can answer "no" to the question. If you're asked if you've ever been convicted of a felony but your DUI was a misdemeanor, then you can also answer "no." On the other hand, if the employer asks you directly if you've ever had a DUI, then you need to tell the employer about any DUIs you've had.

WARNING

Read the question carefully before you answer about DUIs. You may be able to avoid disclosing it. But at the same time, don't lie. Employers will eventually find out.

Tidying up your social media profile

Most employers won't admit to doing this, but they check out your social media profiles on Facebook, Twitter, Instagram, and similar sites.

If you use Facebook and have any questionable posts, you can remove them by looking them up and selecting Delete from the drop-down menu on the upper right of the post. You can go back through your old tweets and do the same on Twitter.

Social media posts that are good candidates for removal include those that contain:

>> Cursing or other offensive language

>> Bragging about partying too much

>> Anything having to do with drugs or alcohol

>> Anything sexual in nature or having to do with nudity

This may seem excessive, but you never know how employers will react to your posts. They may have no business looking at your profile, but you don't want your social media posts to be the one thing that stands between you and your first job.

Making Facebook, Twitter, and Instagram more private

You can also adjust your Facebook, Twitter, and Instagram settings to ensure that your posts are seen only by your friends and to make it harder for employers to find your profile.

To make your Facebook profile more private, follow these steps:

1. **Go to www.facebook.com.**

2. **On the upper right, open the drop-down menu and select Settings.**

3. **On the Settings page, click Privacy in the menu on the left.**

   You land on the Privacy Settings and Tools page, shown in Figure 7-8, where you can control key privacy features.

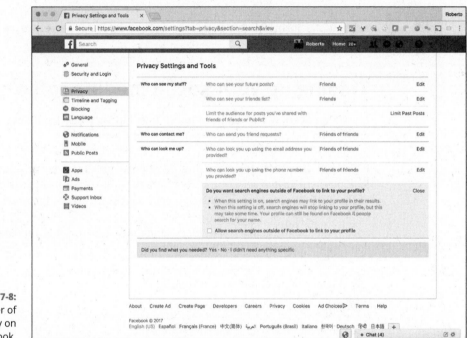

FIGURE 7-8:
Adding a layer of privacy on Facebook.

These are the settings you'll want to change:

>> **Who can see your future posts?** Set this to "Friends."

>> **Who can see your friends list?** Set this to "Friends."

>> **Who can look you up using your email address and phone?** Set these to "Friends of friends." If you have friends in common with employers, they'll still be able to find you. And they can still find you if they type in your name on Facebook.

> **» Do you want search engines outside of Facebook to link to your profile?**
> Set this to "No." Employers may still find you by searching for your name on Facebook, but this step means at least your Facebook profile won't show up in a Google search.

On Twitter, you can update your privacy settings by following these steps:

1. Go to www.twitter.com and log in to your account.

2. In the upper-right corner, click your profile image and in the menu that appears, click Settings and Privacy.

3. From the menu on the left, click Privacy and Safety.

4. Under Photo Tagging, check Do Not Allow Anyone to Tag Me in Photos.

5. Under Discoverability, uncheck Let Others Find Me by My Email Address and Let Others Find Me by My Phone Number.

   Again, as with Facebook, they'll still be able to find you by searching for your name.

6. When you're done, click Save Changes at the bottom of the page.

To protect your privacy on Instagram, follow these steps:

1. Go to www.instagram.com and log into your account.

2. Go to your Instagram profile.

3. If you want, you can temporarily disable your account by clicking the Temporarily Disable My Account link.

   If you don't want to disable your account, instead you can make your account private. Just log in to the app on your phone, access the settings, and toggle the Private Account switch on.

Removing questionable pictures

The same rule that applies to removing questionable posts applies to removing potentially incriminating pictures. You can easily do this on Facebook, Twitter, and Instagram. But you may also show up in photos posted by others, as tends to be the case with Facebook. You may not be able to remove the picture but you can untag yourself.

To untag yourself from a Facebook photo or to delete it, do the following:

1. Go to www.facebook.com.

2. Locate your profile and click Photos.

3. Go to the photo where you want to untag yourself.

4. Click Options on the lower right of the photo.

5. Click Remove Tag if the picture was posted by someone else or Delete This Photo if you took the photo.

TIP

If someone else posted the photo in question and even after untagging yourself, you're concerned someone will see the image, you can ask the person to remove the photo entirely.

To remove yourself from a photo on Twitter, find the offending photo on Twitter and click on it to enlarge it. At the bottom of the photo, you'll see a menu. Click the down-arrow item in the menu to the far right. Then click Remove Your Tag from Photo to remove yourself from the tweet.

You can also go under "Privacy and safety" in your Twitter account and select Do Not Allow Anyone to Tag Me in Photos to prevent people from tagging you.

To untag yourself from a photo on Instagram, tap the photo, tap your name, tap More Options, tap Remove Me from Post, and tap Remove. If you want to leave the tags on the photos but just hide them from your profile, you can go to the Instagram settings, tap Photos of You, and tap Hide Photos to select the ones you want to hide.

Getting rid of controversial tweets

Twitter tends to be more of an open platform with most users choosing to keep their profiles and tweets public for anyone to see. If you have a Twitter account and keep it public, take inventory to make sure you don't have anything offensive.

Political statements, for example, can get you in hot water. So if you've bashed Hillary Clinton or Donald Trump on Twitter lately, your future employer may take notice. Your tweets shouldn't matter and you have the right to free speech. But unfortunately, humans have biases, and incendiary political comments may count against you.

Your options:

>> Stand your ground and don't do anything.

>> Remove any potentially incendiary tweets.

>> Make your Twitter account private.

To make your Twitter account private, follow these steps:

1. Go to `www.twitter.com` and log in.

2. On the upper-right of the screen, click your account icon to bring up the settings menu.

3. Click Settings and Privacy.

4. Click on Privacy and Safety on the left.

5. Check the Protect My Tweets box.

   This will make all your future tweets private. Only your followers will be able to see them. If your previous tweets were retweeted by other people in the past, they'll still be out there.

Choosing an appropriate email address

After your name, your email address is the main thing employers see when they're communicating with you. So make it a good one. Or better yet, don't make it a bad one.

Here are some tips on how to pick a good email address:

>> **Use your first and last name.** If that username is taken, you can use variations. In my case, for example, I can try rangulo, r.angulo, roberto.angulo, or robertoangulo. If your name is something common like John Smith, all those variations may be taken. In that case, you can add a number, like robertoangulo1.

   Don't use digits in place of letters (for example, using the number 1 in place of the letter l), because those look too similar and might result in typos.

>> **Avoid funny names.** If your nickname is Tequila Bob or Cooler because you can pack a lot of beers, don't use that in your username. Try to keep it serious or semiserious. A username like "partymama" may take you out of the running for the job.

TIP

The same rule of keeping your email username serious or semiserious applies to your social media handles. Make sure you update these if they need to be sanitized.

» **Don't include a year.** You don't want to show your age if you're older and you don't want to remind the employer that you're a kid if you were born in the late 1990s or 2000s. It's better to keep your birth year out of your email username.

» **Use Gmail or a custom domain.** If you have a Yahoo! email account, you may be perceived as being behind the times. Gmail is the top email provider and one of the newer ones. If you can get a your own domain name and an email associated with it, that's even cooler than Gmail.

Universities often give alumni email accounts, such as @stanfordalumni.org. If your alumni association offers these accounts, take advantage of it. Having an alumni email address gives you prestige.

When you have your email account, put it on your résumé and use it for all your correspondence with prospective employers.

3
Navigating the Application Process

Chapter **8**

Preparing Your Résumé and Cover Letter

Your résumé is the first thing an employer sees. It sets the recruiter's first impression of you, so you need to make sure your résumé is concise and that it fully reflects what you bring to the organization. No pressure.

Your résumé will pass through automatic screening tools that are looking to filter out irrelevant résumés and select matching ones. It will also be screened quickly by a recruiter, who most likely has piles of dozens of résumés for different positions. Here you learn how to put together a solid résumé that will improve your chances of getting interviews. I cover the basic points that need to be in your résumé and learn tactics that will ensure you stay in the running and don't get weeded out.

Some employers ask for cover letters where you explain why you want to work for the organization. Others see cover letters as a waste of time, and simply ask for your résumé. In this chapter, you also learn how to put together a cover letter that addresses the key points employers want to see.

Your résumé and cover letter can be a doubled-edged sword. They can help or hurt your candidacy. Incorporate the feedback in this chapter to ensure your résumé works for you and not against you.

Writing a Cover Letter

Some employers are more formal than others and will ask you to submit a cover letter as part of your application. The cover letter is your chance to tell the employer why you want to work there and how your experience and background fit with the organization.

It's likely that some of the jobs you apply to will ask you for a cover letter. Here are some best practices to ensure your letter boosts your chances of getting an interview:

>> **Customize it.** Customize your cover letter for each employer and be specific on the role to which you're applying. Employers will notice a cover letter addressed specifically to them. On the flip side, they'll immediately toss an application with a generic cover letter.

>> **Explain why you're a good fit.** This is the main purpose of the cover letter, to explain why the organization should hire you and how your skills and experience matter. If you're applying for a content marketing role, for example, this is where you explain how your writing skills matter. If you can show specific examples of what you've done and how it relates to the job, even better.

>> **Talk about what you bring.** Write about what you bring to the employer and not so much about what the job will do for you. It's okay to write about what you want to get out of the job, but focus on what you can offer.

>> **Pay attention to detail.** Pay close attention to what you write, making sure you spell the employer's name correctly. For example, I've seen candidates apply to AfterCollege and often they'll spell the company name as "Aftercollege" or "After College" or even "AfterSchool." These applications don't make it far. Make sure you get the employer's name right, with the correct punctuation, spaces, and letter capitalization. Pay the same attention to the job title.

>> **Spell check.** This is an obvious one. Yes, you can use spell check, but even this can lead to missed typos. The words *there* and *their*, for example, mean different things but they're often confused and are missed by spell-checking applications.

>> **Proofread.** Have a friend proofread your cover letter. After reading something over and over, your eyes may start skipping over mistakes. If possible, ask someone to look over your work before you send out your letter.

>> **Keep it short.** Just because an employer asks for a cover letter that doesn't mean you need to write an essay. Keep your letter brief and to the point. A half a page is more than enough.

>> **Research the employer.** Make sure your letter says why you want the job. Write about the employer and what you like about it. This can include culture, products, financial performance, or anything along those lines.

TIP

Check out Chapter 4 for a walk-through on how to research prospective employers.

When you know the key elements to include in your cover letter, writing one is easy. Here's an example of how you can write your own:

March 1, 2018

Ms. Jane Smith

Recruiter

State Ranch Insurance Group

543 Main St.

Palo Alto, CA 94305

Dear Ms. Smith:

I am pleased to submit my application for your Claims Analyst position. I graduate in June with a bachelor's degree in finance. As you will see from my résumé, my experience and background match the qualifications listed for the position.

My experience is closely aligned to the responsibilities outlined in the claims analyst role. Most recently, I completed an internship doing financial analysis in the Accounts Payable department of ABC Corp. Although the role was slightly different, the work involved parallels that of your claims analyst role. In my previous internships and part-time work, I was also able to develop the analytical skills and obtain mastery of the software and tools that I may use if I have the privilege of joining your organization.

Academically, I've focused my coursework on finance and analysis. This provides me with the background and knowledge to allow me to quickly ramp up at State Ranch Insurance Group to become a productive member of the team.

Last, I noticed that you're opening an office in Neighboring City USA and you're looking to build out a team in that location. Please know that I am flexible, and given my interested in joining your organization, I'm able to work in either of your two locations.

I welcome the opportunity to discuss this position and will contact you in the coming days to follow up. If there is additional information you would like from me, please let me know. I am excited at the prospect of joining State Ranch Insurance Group and look forward to contributing as a productive member of your team.

Thank you for your consideration.

Use your cover letter to highlight things that are not covered in your résumé. Don't use it to rehash what the employer can already find in your résumé.

Creating a Great Résumé

Your résumé, also referred to sometimes as your CV (short for *curriculum vitae*), is the most important component of the application. It's also one of the parts of the process with which many new job seekers struggle. But don't worry. Here you get a quick overview on how to put together your résumé and what to include in it.

You can create your résumé in a variety or formats. I recommend you use Microsoft Word because it's the predominant application in the business world and is most likely what a recruiter will use. Other tools exist, like Google Docs. I love Google Docs for collaborating with others or sharing documents, but when it comes to preparing a nicely formatted document, Microsoft Word is still the tool to use. This is especially true when writing your résumé.

You can buy a discounted copy of Microsoft Office with a valid student identification. You can also find computers at libraries or school computer clusters with Microsoft Office installed.

Formatting your résumé

Lets start with the actual document structure. Formatting your résumé is important for a couple of reasons:

>> **It makes it easier for the recruiter to read it.** A well-formatted résumé can make the difference between your getting to the next stage or not.

>> **It makes it easier for your résumé to be read by software that lets employers screen applications.** Employers rely more and more on computer algorithms to sort and match résumés to available jobs. Making your résumé searchable by these algorithms will increase your chances of getting the job.

Do the following to make your résumé more likely to be picked by a recruiter or by a machine:

>> **Stick to simple fonts.** The most commonly used fonts are Times New Roman, Arial, Helvetica, Georgia, and Garamond. Try to stick to one of these when writing your résumé. Without getting into specifics of how fonts work, these fonts are the most common, and most computers have them. Don't use exotic or rare fonts, because these can come out as symbols on other computers, making your résumé illegible.

>> **Use reverse chronological order.** This is a fancy way of saying "list your most common experience and education first." This tends to be the norm, and recruiters are used to seeing certain things at certain points in a résumé. By sticking to this order, you ensure that recruiters are looking at the information you want to highlight.

>> **Align to the left.** Most recruiters are used to reading résumés from left to right. So make sure you align your résumé accordingly. You could align it to the right and be original, but again, you want to make it easy for the recruiter to read about your experience and education. The same goes for the scanning machine that may read your résumé. It will most likely expect your résumé to be aligned to the left.

>> **Start with an objective.** The objective should be the first section of your résumé. If this is your first job out of college, then the next section should be your education, followed by experience, and then followed by any specific skills or accomplishments.

If you have experience that is more relevant than your education, put the experience section of your résumé above the one that covers your education.

TIP

>> **Use white or light color paper.** The most common color is white. You can also use an off-white or light-cream colored paper. Unless you're applying to a role where you really need to show off your creativity, stick to the most common colors.

Avoiding common mistakes

Don't get too preoccupied with making your résumé perfect. There's no one right way to write one. As long as you follow basic formatting advice, you're in good shape.

Here are some things you should avoid. These are not necessarily death traps, but practices you can avoid to ensure your résumé makes it through to the next step:

TIP

>> **Don't go over one page.** Given that you're looking for your first job, you most likely have the right amount of experience and education that will fit on one page. Most employers look for one-page résumés, so do your best to keep it that way. If you have a PhD or a number of publications under your name, then you may need to add a second or third page.

If you have a two-page résumé, print it on two sheets of paper and not on a two-sided sheet. This way, you ensure the recruiter will see the second sheet and not overlook it by not flipping over to the other side of your résumé. Also make sure to add your name to the second page and add page numbers.

>> **Don't use pictures.** In many countries, it's common practice to include your photo on your résumé. This is not the case in the United States. Don't include a photo, no matter how good looking or handsome you are. It doesn't add value to your application, and it may actually get you eliminated, because employers are under pressure to make unbiased hiring decisions that avoid discrimination.

>> **Don't use the paper that's in your printer.** Paper résumés are becoming less common and are being replaced by online résumés. But in cases where you're asked to bring a paper copy, make sure you use good paper. The most common type of paper that you find in copiers and printers is 20-pound paper. This is good enough for everyday printing, but not for your résumé. This paper tends to be flimsy and it crumples easily. Instead, use 24-pound paper. It's a bit thicker and will last longer.

Identifying key résumé elements

Your résumé can consist of four to six key elements, some of which are optional while others are required.

Contact information

This is an obvious one, but it's key. Always include your email address and your phone number. You want to make sure the employer is able to contact you about next steps.

TIP

Unless the employer specifically asks for this, don't include your mailing address on your résumé. If you're applying to a job in another city, the employer may eliminate you if it can find a candidate similar to you locally.

Objective

The objective is an optional element, but you should include it. Be specific and mention the role to which you're applying. An example of an objective can be:

> To secure a role as an ER nurse at a top healthcare facility.

Education

Education is usually the next element in a résumé, especially for entry-level job seekers. List your college or university. You can also include your high school or preparatory school if it's a well-known one.

Coursework

This section is optional. You normally don't include classes you've taken in your résumé. The big exception is with technical roles. Sometimes, employers look to hire candidates who've taken specific courses in some programming languages or from certain professors. If you know of an employer looking for this information, add it to your résumé.

Skills

This section is also optional. Only add skills if you have specific programming knowledge or possess a skill that is high in demand.

Languages

If you speak any languages fluently, besides English, list them here. You never know — an employer may value this skill even if it's not specified in the job description.

Grade point average

The grade point average (GPA) is another optional piece. Some employers ask for your GPA; others don't. Add your GPA if it's higher than 3.5 or the equivalent on a different scale. Don't include it if it's lower than this.

TIP

If you need to include your GPA and it's not high enough, calculate your GPA in your major to see if it's higher than your overall GPA. If it is, then include that instead.

Experience

This tends to be the hardest section for first-time job seekers. You may find your-self in a Catch-22 if a job asks for experience, but you need a first job in order to get this experience. This is where you list your internships and any part-time job that relates to the role to which you're applying. Include activities where you've played a key role and achieved some outcome that generated results. For example, if you were a volunteer for a fundraising event and played a key role in raising a significant amount of funds, include this in your experience. As another example, if you were in a sorority or fraternity and helped recruit a certain number of mem-bers, add this here, especially if you're applying to a sales or marketing role.

TIP

Check out Chapter 2 to get ideas on what to add to the experience section of your résumé.

Activities and honors

Here you include any awards or honors you've received. If you were a member of an honor society or fraternity or sorority, add it here. Do you do community ser-vice or have any special hobbies such as climbing or running? Include these activi-ties here if there's room on your résumé. These items show a part of who you are. Employers like to see this. They may also establish a connection with any of the people interviewing you later on if they were members of the same group or if they like similar activities.

Using action words

Action words denote achievement and make your résumé look better. Use them throughout your résumé, including under any bulleted lists that describe what you did at a previous job or in any of your activities.

For example, instead of writing:

> Was responsible for managing account payables

You should write:

> Managed account payables

Writing your résumé in an action-oriented way adds more importance to your responsibilities and will cause the employer to take notice.

Here is a compilation of common action verbs you can include in your résumé:

Communication Skills

Addressed

Advertised

Authored

Clarified

Consulted

Convinced

Corresponded

Debated

Defined

Directed

Discussed

Edited

Elicited

Enlisted

Explained

Expressed

Formulated

Incorporated

Influenced

Interacted

Interpreted

Interviewed

Listened

Presented

Promoted

Proposed

Publicized

Reconciled

Reported

Suggested

Summarized

Translated

Wrote

Research Skills

Analyzed

Calculated

Collected

Compared

Detected

Determined

Diagnosed

Evaluated

Formulated

Gathered

Inspected

Organized

Prepared

Reviewed

Solved

Summarized

Surveyed

Helping Skills

Advocated

Aided

Answered

Arranged

Assessed

Assisted

Contributed

Cooperated

Counseled

Demonstrated

Ensured

Expedited

Facilitated

Helped

Prevented

Provided

Referred

Supplied

Volunteered

Management Skills

Administered

Attained

Chaired

Considered

Directed

Eliminated

Emphasized

Enforced

Enhanced

Established

Executed

Generated

Handled

Headed

Hired

Implemented

Improved

Incorporated

Informed

Led

Maintained

Mediated

Monitored

Motivated

Oversaw

Scheduled

Secured

Selected

Streamlined

Strengthened

Creative Skills

Acted

Adapted

Authored

Began

Combined

Composed

Conceptualized

Condensed

Created

Established	Coached
Formulated	Communicated
Founded	Conducted
Illustrated	Coordinated
Initiated	Critiqued
Instituted	Developed
Integrated	Educated
Introduced	Enabled
Invented	Encouraged
Modified	Evaluated
Originated	Explained
Performed	Facilitated
Photographed	Familiarized
Planned	Focused
Revised	Guided
Revitalized	Individualized
Shaped	Persuaded
	Taught
Teaching Skills	Tested
Adapted	Trained
Advised	
Clarified	

Looking at a sample résumé

The résumé shown in Figure 8-1 incorporates many of the concepts described in terms of formatting, adding key elements, and using action verbs.

TIP

When you create a résumé and style it as you like, save it as a PDF. This format is good for sending to others because it lets them see your résumé as you'd like them to see it.

```
Anna Garcia
1200 Main St.
Boston, MA 02102
(617) 555-5555
agarcia@nurseuniversity.edu

OBJECTIVE
To obtain a position in a Registered Nurse New Grad Program.

EDUCATION
Nurse University, September 2004 to present                    Boston, MA
Bachelor of Science in Nursing, degree anticipated May 2018.

Relevant course work includes:
  ▪ Basic concepts in critical care nursing, management, and leadership.

Nursing school clinicals:
  ▪ Community mental health rotation, pediatric rotation, maternity rotation, labor and
    delivery and post-partum units, med./surg. rotation, telemetry and medical-surgical units.

EXPERIENCE
Hospital C, January 2017 to present                           Boston, MA
Fifth Semester Preceptorship, Pediatric Surgical Unit
  ▪ Accomplished interventions and assessments for 4 patients per shift.
  ▪ Prioritized multiple tasks.
  ▪ Provided IV therapy, blood transfusions, NG feeding, wound care, catheter insertion and
    removal, IV insertion and removal.
  ▪ Utilized translation skills.

Hospital D, June 2016 to September 2016                       Boston, MA
Intern
  ▪ Provided total care to patients with guidance from preceptor in SICU and  MICU.
  ▪ Acquired critical nursing, time management, and critical thinking skills.

Hospital E, January 2016 to April 2016                        Boston, MA
Volunteer
  ▪ Performed various duties on post-partum floor that included filing, managing records,
    coordinating activities, and attending to patients.

PROFESSIONAL AFFILIATIONS AND CERTIFICATIONS
  ▪ Sigma Theta Tau International Honor Society of Nursing, September 2016 to present
  ▪ Student Nursing Association, September 2016 to present
  ▪ CPR Certification, current.

SKILLS
  ▪ Excellent written and oral communication skills
  ▪ Proficient computer skills, including Microsoft Office

ADDITIONAL INFORMATION
  ▪ Fluent in Spanish and French
```

FIGURE 8-1:
Sample résumé.

Getting Résumé Help

When you have a first draft of your résumé ready, ask for a second pair of eyes to review it.

Taking your résumé to your college career center

Your school's career center can be of great help in writing and improving your résumé. Stop by or schedule an appointment to meet with a career counselor and ask for assistance.

When I was in college, I remember meeting with a counselor who was able to look at my résumé and provide pointers on how to make it more appealing. It took an hour from my day to go to the career center, but the amount of time I saved in trying to figure out how to improve my résumé was worth it.

Using TopResume to improve your résumé

Another way to go is to enlist the help of a professional writing service to make your résumé stand out. These services usually charge a fee, but it may be very well worth it if you think your résumé can be improved.

One of these services is TopResume. It's one of the best ones out there and also one of the largest. Check out TopResume by going to www.topresume.com.

Chapter **9**

Applying for Jobs

The actual process of applying for a job can be cumbersome. Some jobs require you to apply in person. For other jobs, you need to email a résumé and cover letter. But for most jobs these days, you need to fill out long online application forms. The more jobs you apply to, the more different systems you'll encounter. The process is not complicated, but it can be tedious.

More and more employers rely on applicant tracking systems (ATSs) to handle a huge volume of applicants. These systems are supposed to save employers time and help them with record keeping. For job seekers, though, these disparate systems often create more work, which makes it harder to stand out.

In this chapter, you get insights on how to get your application noticed. You also get tips on how to get visibility into the process and the status of your candidacy.

Applying for a job should be simple. With some basic planning and a little patience, you'll breeze through this process.

Starting the Application Process

Now that you're ready to begin applying for jobs, it's time to do some basic planning. As you find jobs of interest, create a list of them so you can track your progress.

This can be a simple list that you can create in Microsoft Excel or Google Docs. Instead of applying for jobs as you find them, compile your list and then submit applications for these jobs in batches. This helps to time job offers so you can better compare and evaluate them once the time comes.

TIP

Here is a blank Google Sheet you can copy and use as your own: http://bit.ly/2gDw6Qm.

As you add jobs you like to your list, note the URL of where you need to go to find the job again and where you need to apply. At the same time, look for people you know at each of the employers of interest.

TIP

Employee referrals go a long way toward helping you get a job, so don't rely purely on sending in online applications.

Other things to keep in mind as you apply for work:

>> **Don't apply to every job under the sun.** This is especially true when applying to a number of jobs with the same employer. Be focused. Apply to one type of job at a particular employer. For example, you can apply for a software developer role and an application developer role at the same organization, as these are both similar. You can also apply to the same job but at different locations. On the other hand, if you apply for completely different types of jobs at the same organization, you come off as being unfocused and not clear in what you want to do. This can count against you. HR people refer to people who do this as "serial applicants."

>> **Be ready to customize your résumé.** Yes, you have to. You've spent a good amount of time on your résumé and cover letter. To make your application more effective, though, you'll need to at least change your objective to match the job in question. Most jobs also ask for a cover letter. A generic one won't cut it. You should create a different cover letter for each job, explaining why you're interested in the position and how you're qualified for it.

>> **Apply via job boards.** Most jobs you find on job boards either redirect you to the employer's applicant tracking system (ATS) or make you apply on the job board. Take advantage and apply via the job board and don't go to the employer's ATS directly, as many job seekers do. If you apply via the job board, you'll be redirected to the ATS anyway, where you can apply. But the added benefit of the job board is that it also keeps track of your application, and often the job board will report the applications it generates to the employers. This increases your chances of getting noticed by the employer.

Using Applicant Tracking Systems

ATSs are a necessary evil when applying for a job. Most large employers use them and you'll most likely have to fill out applications on a different ATS for each employer. Be ready to invest some time into this process.

Here are some ways you can make the most out of applying via an ATS:

» **Create an account.** If given the option to apply as a guest or to create a login and password, definitely create an account. This allows you to save your work and go back later if needed. You can also make updates to your application. Last and most important, you'll be able to log on after you apply and check the status of your application. Not all ATSs do this, but many of the large ones do.

» **Join the talent community.** Some employers have "talent communities" or "talent networks" built into their ATSs. By joining an employer's talent network, you're giving the employer permission to email you about other opportunities and recruiting events. Recruiters at the organization may also reach out to you on occasion. If given the option to join an employer's talent network or subscribe to updates, do it. This is a good way to stay on the employer's radar and for you to learn about other opportunities in case you don't get the job to which you applied.

» **Upload a résumé.** ATSs often give you the choice to upload a résumé file, enter your résumé via an online form, or apply via your LinkedIn account. If given the choice, upload a résumé file, preferably in PDF format. This allows you to preserve any formatting in the uploaded file that you've applied to your résumé. It's also a faster option because the ATS will read in all the data in your résumé and add it to the appropriate fields in the ATS.

WARNING

Double-check the fields in the application form to ensure that the data in your uploaded résumé file made it to the right form fields correctly.

» **Avoid leaving blank fields.** The more data you fill out on the ATS, the more likely you are to be found by a recruiter at the organization to which you're applying. Select all relevant skills you have from any drop-down, upload files of your past work if given the option, and enter keywords when asked, because these are searchable fields.

All these steps will help you get noticed by the recruiter at the organization.

Finding Someone to Refer You

Employee referrals are among the most effective ways to get a job. Finding someone to introduce you to the employer will boost your chances of getting the job. At a minimum, it will get you a phone interview.

When you know where you want to apply, start by asking family members if they know anyone who works at the organizations that interest you. Next, ask your friends and classmates. Do you know a professor or teaching assistant who knows people at a certain organization? Ask for an introduction.

Tapping alumni from your school

If you don't know anyone first hand, you can contact school alumni who work at employers that interest you and ask them for referrals. Not all alumni may be able or willing to help, but you'll find that many will offer a helping hand.

Go to your alumni association or your local alumni group and ask for help. Alumni associations sometimes have mentoring programs where they put you in touch with alumni who can give you advice. At a minimum, they should be able to introduce you to alumni contacts. You can also contact alumni via LinkedIn. To find contacts via LinkedIn, follow these steps:

1. Go to www.linkedin.com.

2. Start typing your school's name in the search box on the upper left of the page.

3. Click the school name.

   You're taken to your school's page on LinkedIn.

4. Scroll down until you get to the "Career Insights" section and then click See All Career Insights.

   You're taken to the Career Insights page for your school.

5. Search for alumni who work at a specific organization, and narrow by graduation year, as shown in Figure 9-1.

Find alumni who are most relevant to the role you're pursuing. You can send them a simple message along these lines:

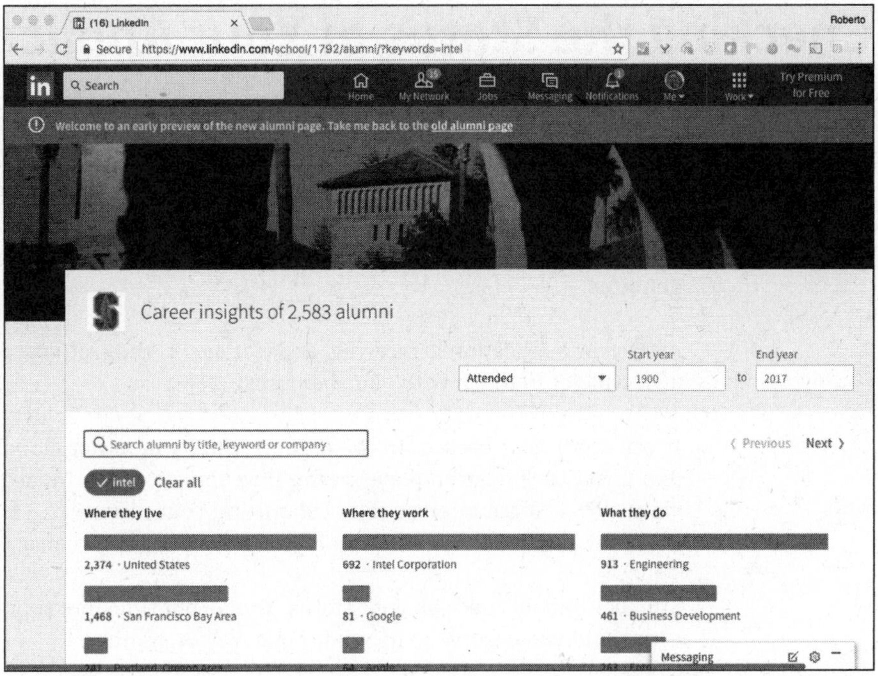

FIGURE 9-1:
The LinkedIn
Career Insights
page for a sample
university.

Hi,

I'm a student or recent graduate studying _____ at your alma mater. I'm very interested in a _____ role in your organization. Would you be willing to talk to me for 10 to 15 minutes about the organization and your experience?

Sincerely,

You may not hear back, but sending these messages is worth a shot. If you hear back from the alum, take the call with her and ask her about the organization. Also tell her about yourself.

Make it a goal to have a good conversation, and if you think the call goes well, then ask her if she can refer you to the organization.

REMEMBER

Asking for assistance is hard. If an alum responds to you, it means she's willing to help. Take advantage of the opportunity and be thankful! Alumni have been in your shoes and are often willing to pay it forward.

Referrals help get you in the door. Your contact doesn't need to endorse you on LinkedIn. Just let the recruiter know that you've applied and to be on the lookout for your application. Even that will make a difference.

Checking the Status of Your Application

When you apply to a job, a recruiter within the organization will usually see your résumé first and then direct it to the relevant hiring manager for the position. The recruiter tends to be someone in human resources who helps recruit for the organization. The term *hiring manager* refers to the person who needs to hire, and the one who created the position. This person will most likely be your boss if you get hired.

After your application is received, and if it's a fit, the recruiter or the hiring manager will get in touch with you about next steps.

If you don't hear back from the organization, you're not alone. Most job seekers don't hear back from employers after they apply for jobs. In fact, applying for a job via an ATS is often referred to as submitting your résumé to a black hole. So if you don't get any news from the employer, don't despair, because you're not alone.

Still, you should check on your status. You've put time into submitting your application and you deserve to hear back one way or another.

Most ATSs ask you to create a login and password when first applying for a job. These login credentials allow you to go back later to check on how your application is going. Each system varies, but in general, they allow you to see the jobs to which you've applied and see any data that the employer has entered. The job listing may appear as "Active," as shown in Figure 9-2. This means no hire has been made yet or hires have been made but the position is still open because there may be more than one opening for the specific role.

A job listing can also appear as "Closed" or "Filled." If you haven't heard anything from the recruiter, it's safe to assume the position has been filled and you didn't get the job.

TIP

If it's been a couple weeks since you applied for a job via email, in person, or via an ATS and don't know your status, you should definitely reach out to the recruiter to check on the status of your application. Just call the recruiter or email him to ask if he received your application. It's that simple. The three key things you need to know are:

>> Did he receive your application and is everything in order?

>> Has your application been reviewed?

>> When can you expect to hear back about next steps, or about no next steps?

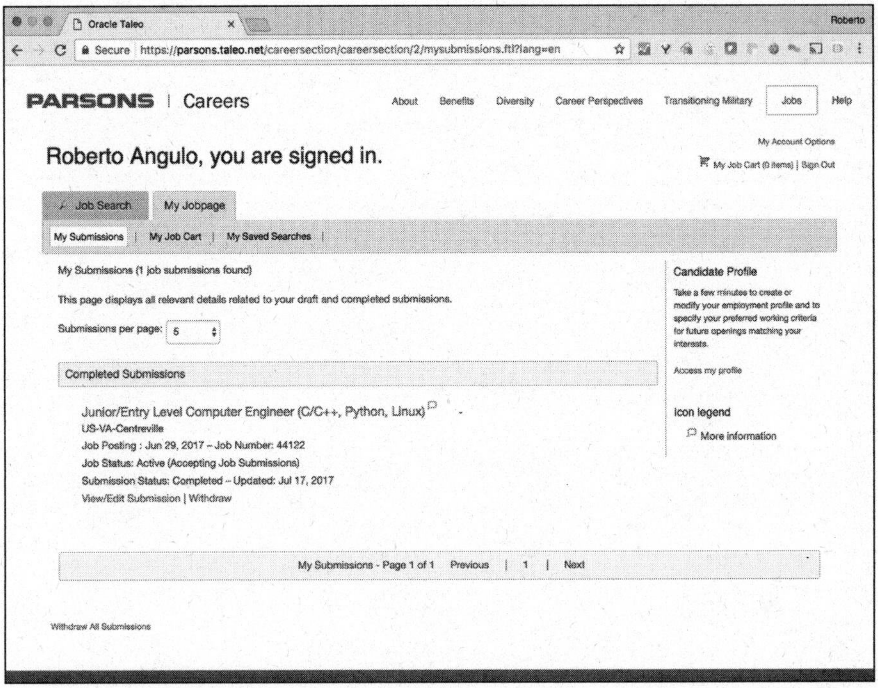

FIGURE 9-2:
A sample applicant tracking system (ATS) showing the status of an application.

Here's a sample email you can send to the recruiter:

> Hello,
>
> I recently applied for the _____ position at your organization. I'm checking to see if you received my application and if everything is in order. I look forward to hearing from you on next steps, as I am very interested in the role and in your organization.
>
> Sincerely,

You may not hear back from the recruiter, but it's still worth reaching out. At worst, your message will go unanswered. At best, it raises awareness of your application, and it shows you're interested in the job. Plus, if for some reason your application was not received, you have a chance to resubmit it.

TIP

If you applied to a job online and don't have the recruiter's contact information, look for contact information on the organization's career page. Also try emailing jobs@ or careers@ and then the company's domain. For example, jobs@google.com or careers@visa.com. You can also go on LinkedIn and search for people with recruiter titles within the organization and reach out to them.

4

Acing the Interview and Getting the Offer You Want

Do your homework on the employer and on those you meet with so you can be confident and do well in your interview.

Follow simple etiquette guidelines that help you make a good first impression and further strengthen your candidacy for the job.

Be ready for tough questions and get through these easily without letting them become stumbling blocks.

Prioritize what's important to you and work accordingly to get the job offer you want.

Turn an offer down without burning bridges.

Weigh the pros and cons of job offers in different cities by taking housing and other relevant factors into account.

Chapter **10**

Before the Interview

Landing your first interview is a big step in your quest for the right job. You've figured out what kind of job you want, you know where you want to work, and you've searched for and applied to jobs that interest you. Now you need to make sure you do well in your interviews so you get a job offer. The job interview process may seem daunting. Recent grads say this is one of the most difficult parts of the job search. With some preparation and knowledge, you won't have to worry about your interviews.

In this chapter, I fill you in on resources to help you research employers and their industries. I also explain the various types of interviews, the steps involved, and the different stakeholders.

Just as important as the interview is the channel through which it is conducted. In this chapter, I provide an overview of some popular interview tools and technologies so you can better prepare if you're interviewing virtually.

This chapter arms you with the tools you need to prepare for your interview and go in with confidence.

Preparing for Your Interview

A little preparation goes a long way. To start, find out as much as you can about the organization you're interviewing with. Learn its history and its mission, and become familiar with its products, services, and activities. Get acquainted with the management team to see whom you may know. This information will allow you to ask thoughtful questions during the interview, which will impress the interviewer.

You also need to know whom you're interviewing with. Are you interviewing with your future boss? With a potential colleague? Or with a recruiter? This information will help decide whether you need to research the person in question or focus more on showcasing yourself in order to make it past the first interview.

REMEMBER

Often, your enthusiasm and interest in the organization are just as important as what you bring to the table. So be sure to do your homework prior to your interview!

Starting with the employer's website

An employer's website — especially if it's a medium to large employer — often provides all the information you need to know. Go to the about page — you should see a link at the top or bottom of the page. Figure 10-1 shows an example of an about page; this one is for the National Renewable Energy Laboratory (NREL), an energy-focused research organization based in Colorado. There you can find the history of the organization, a description of products and services, and any noteworthy information that the organization is highlighting.

FIGURE 10-1:
An example of an about page.

Depending on the organization, you may also find a news page with featured articles and press releases. Figure 10-2 shows NREL's news page (called "Newsroom"), with announcements that the organization deems newsworthy.

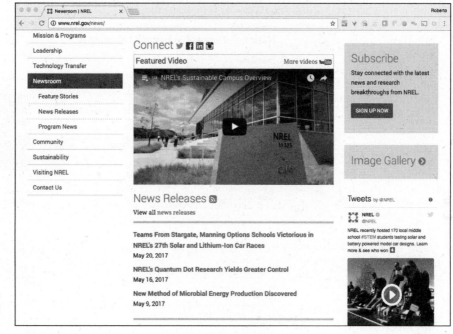

FIGURE 10-2:
An example of
a news page.

Read the news page carefully and become familiar with the announcements highlighted here. They're almost sure to be a topic of conversation during your interview.

The more you know about the organization, the better the impression you will make.

REMEMBER

Using Wikipedia to research the employer

While the employer's site is a great source of information, it's also biased to what the organization wants you to see. Another great place to research employers is Wikipedia. Wikipedia is a crowdsourced encyclopedia, meaning that the contributions come from the public. Here, you can get more insight into the organization and a comprehensive perspective from various points of view.

Figure 10-3 shows an example of NREL's Wikipedia page. Here you can see a short summary of the organization, a snapshot of when NREL was founded, and its budget. As you scroll down you can see a history and read more about its areas of focus. Almost all Wikipedia entries include a reference section, where you can take a deeper look at the sources of information.

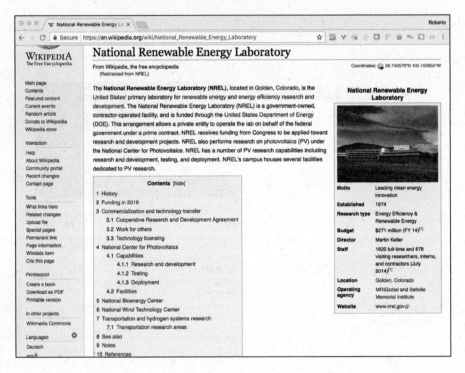

FIGURE 10-3:
The Wikipedia page for NREL.

REMEMBER

Not all employers have Wikipedia entries, but you should still look to make sure.

Finding competing companies on Owler

Owler (www.owler.com) is a great place to find out about an employer's competitors and similar organizations (see Figure 10-4). Looking up these other organizations gives you perspective on the sector in which the employer operates. It also makes you aware of other organizations to which you may want to apply.

TIP

You'll need to enter your email address to access data on Owler. You'll receive daily email updates on the employers you look up on Owler.

The site also pulls third-party news references about an employer, such as tweets and articles that mention the organization, as shown in Figure 10-5. Take a look at these news articles to get additional insight on the organization prior to your interview.

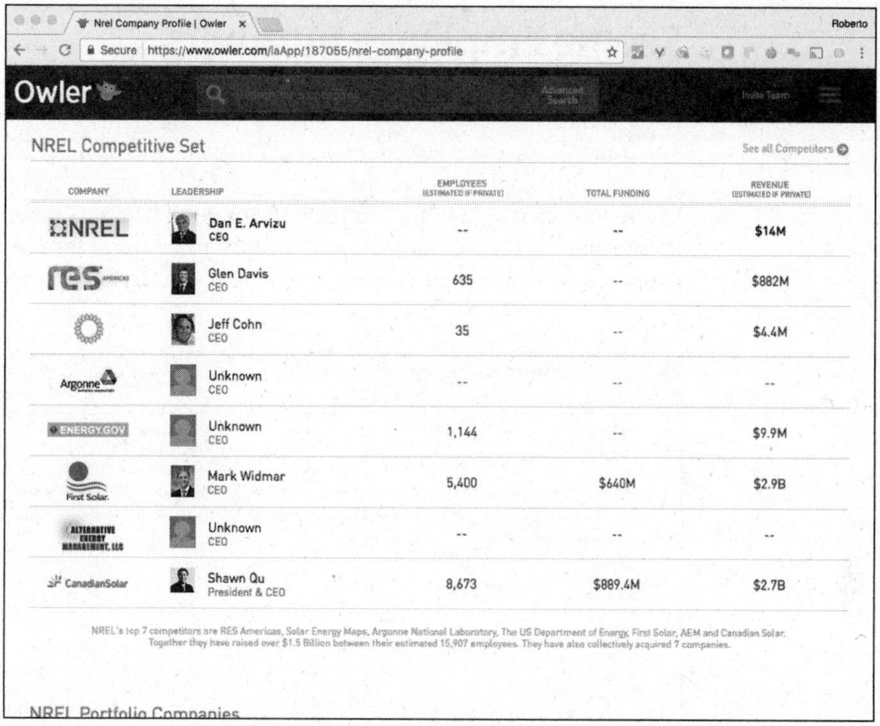

FIGURE 10-4:
The competitive
set for NREL
on Owler.

FIGURE 10-5:
News about NREL
on Owler.

Seeing employer numbers on Yahoo! Finance

The Yahoo! Finance section (http://finance.yahoo.com) lets you look at the finances of companies that are publicly listed on one of the stock exchanges. If you're interviewing with a company that's public, go to Yahoo! Finance to look at its stock price. Figure 10-6 shows the stock price trend for the past year for Raytheon, an aerospace and defense company and a large employer.

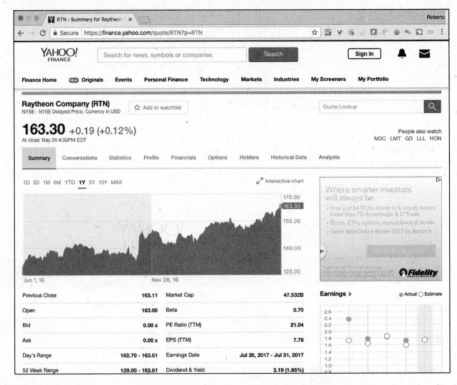

FIGURE 10-6: Checking a company's stock price on Yahoo! Finance.

If the company's stock price was once high and has been trending down, you should take this as a red flag. On the other hand, if the company's stock has been trending upward, that's a sign the company is doing well.

TIP

To see a company's stock price trend, click 1Y to see the past year's data. Click 5Y to see the past five years' data.

Click Financials to see how much revenue the company generates, its cost structure, and whether it's making or losing money (see Figure 10-7). You can even see how much cash the company has in the bank and how much debt it has. Some debt is good, but if a company has a lot of debt, little cash, and is losing money, that may be a red flag.

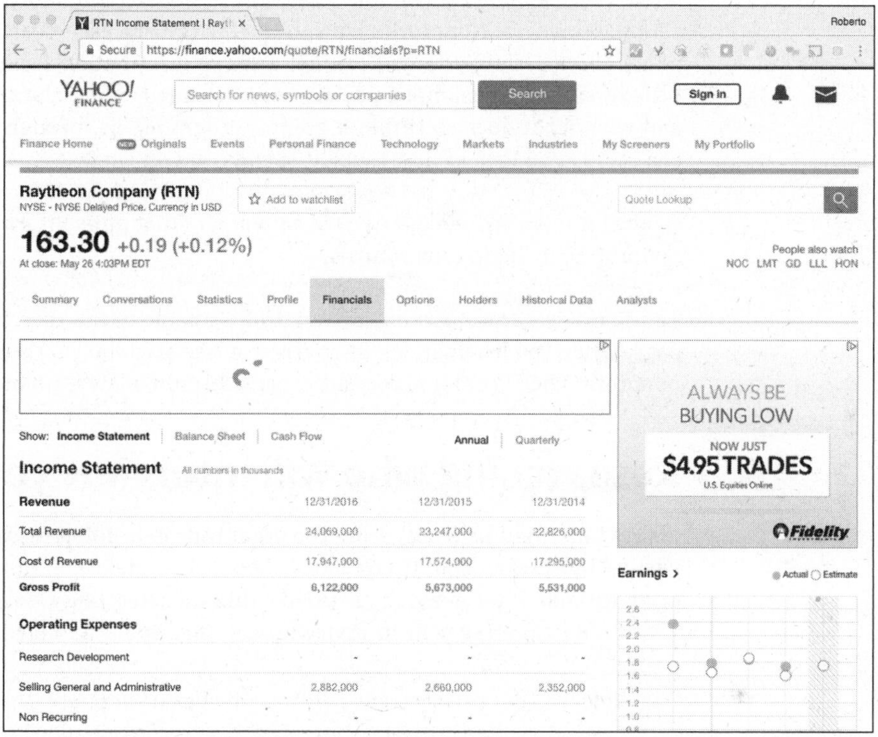

FIGURE 10-7:
Checking a company's income statement and related data on Yahoo! Finance.

You will see the company's income statement with revenue, which is also sales. The net income will be a positive number if the company is generating a profit or negative if the company is losing money.

To see the company's cash in the bank and debt, click Financials and then click Balance Sheet. "Cash and Cash Equivalents" shows how much cash the company has; "Long-Term Debt" and "Short-Term Debt" show how much debt the company has.

Having a good picture of the company's finances helps you gain a better perspective on the organization and may inform your final decision on whether you ultimately join the company if given an offer. It will also prompt you to ask questions during the interview about why, for example, the company's sales have gone up or why the company has taken on debt, if that's the case.

Digging into a nonprofit's finances via GuideStar

If you're interviewing at a registered nonprofit (and most nonprofits are registered), you can prepare for your interview by getting acquainted with the organization's finances. Nonprofits have to file tax returns each year. These returns are public information, and you can get a lot of information from them by doing a little research. For example, you can see how much money the nonprofit generates and whether it does so through grants, programs, or through investments. You can also get an idea of how much it spends and on what.

GuideStar (www.guidestar.org) is a great site that pulls information together on nonprofits, including tax returns.

To use GuideStar, search for the nonprofit's name in the search box on the home page. When you locate it, log in or create a free account. On the detail page for the nonprofit, click Form 990 to see the organization's latest financial report.

Researching who will interview you

Just as important as researching the organization is doing research on the people who will interview you. If you know their names, take the time to look them up prior to your interviews. You can do this on sites like Google, LinkedIn, and Twitter. Researching your interviewers can give you the following data points:

>> **Role:** You can usually find a person's job title on her public LinkedIn profile. You can also see how long she has been at the organization and if she has had different roles there.

>> **School:** You can see where a person went to school. If you and the interviewer went to the same school, this could be a good conversation topic during your interview because you have something in common.

>> **Interests:** You can get an idea of a person's interest by seeing what groups she belongs to on LinkedIn and what she has liked. If she has a Twitter account, you can also see what types of information she has shared.

To look up a person online, search for the person's name with quotation marks around it and the employer's name, like this: "Roberto Angulo" AfterCollege.

TIP

Adding the name of the employer helps ensure you narrow your search to the person at the organization and to filter out other people with the same name.

As you can see in Figure 10-8, your search results will include a link to the person's LinkedIn profile and other notable mentions.

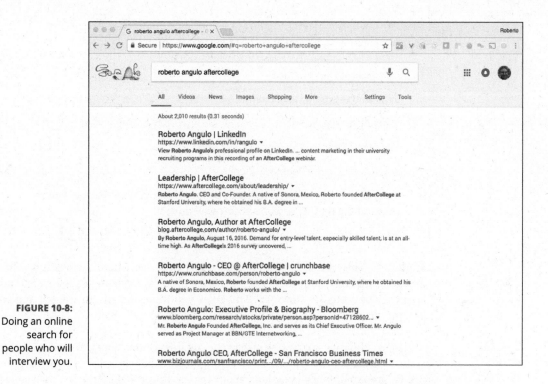

FIGURE 10-8: Doing an online search for people who will interview you.

All these data points will give you a better perspective on the people with whom you'll interview. This will help you to ask questions about their experience at the organization and find common topics for conversation during your interview.

Learning about the job you're applying for

Whether you're interviewing for a job where you'll be the only one with a certain role or where you'll be one of many, you should prepare some questions for your interview that are specific to your prospective job. For example, if you're the only one with your job description, how will you learn and whom will you learn from? If you'll be one of many in the organization with the same role, how do you advance? And what are the typical career paths of someone with your role and how long is the average tenure?

In cases where you'll be one of many, you can usually find this information on LinkedIn. For example, if you're interviewing for an account executive role at Gannett, one of the largest media companies in the United States, you can get a glimpse of other people with the same role.

To find people with a certain role at an organization:

1. **Go to** www.linkedin.com.

2. **Type in the organization name.**

   As you're typing, you should see "People who work at [organization]."

3. **Click the "People who work at . . ." link.**

   You're taken to the People section.

4. **Next to the organization name in the search box, type the role you're researching (in this case, "account executive").**

   You'll see a list of people working at the employer with the specific job title.

From here, you can click on individual profiles to see where various individuals with the same role went to school, their past employer experience if any, and how long they've lasted in the role. This gives you more insight on the job and will prompt you to ask questions during your interview.

If the job is unique and no one else in the organization is doing the same job, look at the original job description. Look through the responsibilities and qualifications and be prepared to ask questions about the employer's expectations for you as it relates to each responsibility.

Practicing for the Interview

Even a little bit of practice goes a long way toward preparing for your interview. To start, assume you'll have anywhere from 30 minutes to an hour with the interviewer, or with each interviewer if there are more than one. This means you need to plan how long you'll spend introducing yourself, for your interview, and for you to ask questions.

TIP

Practice interviewing with a friend or mentor either in person or over the phone, going over some of the questions you think you may be asked.

Here are some things you can practice prior to your interview.

Introducing yourself

Plan on providing a brief overview about yourself, including what you studied and why. Also talk about what you'd like to do in your career, and how the job for which you're interviewing helps you with your journey. Mention why you're excited to be considered for the job.

Here's an example introduction for someone studying economics:

> I just finished my degree in economics from [school name]. I went into this field of study because I wanted to learn about how business works and how it relates to government and society. . .. My ultimate goal is to [your goal — for example, starting a business, running a large company, or being in government]. [Organization name] is at the forefront of [what organization does]. I'm looking to work here as [job title]. I hope to learn about [specific goals] while also contributing to the [growth of organization/advancement of research in a certain field/advancement in mission of organization] and ultimately [your goal].

What to ask

Typically, at the end of the interview you'll be asked if you have any questions. You should definitely have questions ready. Asking about the job or the organization shows you're interested. Not having any questions may put the interviewer off and can be interpreted as lack of interest. Narrow the list of important questions you'd like to ask to five or six. These can be questions about the job, the organization, or the industry. Assume some will be answered during the course of your interview and be ready to ask at least two of them.

Answering questions

Just as important as your answers is how concise you are and whether you can answer the questions well enough while staying focused. Don't stray or give long-winded answers.

Familiarize yourself with the job description before your interview. Go over the responsibilities and think of ways to connect them with your own experience, whether it consists of class projects, part-time work, or volunteer work.

TIP

Employers want to hear why you're eager to join the organization. They also want to know how you'd like to contribute. But because this is your first job, they also expect to hear that you want to learn and grow. Most important, be genuine and make sure you don't sound like you're reading off a script.

Familiarizing Yourself with the Interview Process

One of the best ways to prepare is to have an idea of who you're interviewing with and the format of the interview. The more you know ahead of time, the more comfortable and confident you'll be when you're interviewing.

Here are some of the things you should know prior to your interview:

>> **Location:** Find out where you'll be interviewing. If it's on your college campus, visit the location ahead of time to get familiar with the place and to know how to get there. If it's in another location, check the address on Google Maps ahead of time to see how far it is and how it will take you to get there. Make sure you account for traffic.

>> **Security check:** Many organizations require a valid government ID, such as a driver's license or passport, in order to verify your identity. Make sure you bring your driver's license, a passport, or some other form of identification, with a picture, to your interview. Also ensure that the identification is not expired.

>> **What to bring:** Ask if you need to bring anything to your interview such as a copy of your résumé, references, a sample of your work, or a computer.

>> **Number of interviews and length:** Are you going for one initial interview or will you have a full day of interviewing with various stakeholders? Plan your day accordingly. For example, if your interview starts early in the morning and lasts until noon, make sure you eat breakfast beforehand so that you don't get hungry during your interviews.

TIP

Doing long interviews and talking for extended periods of time can cause you to get thirsty or get dry mouth. Bring a bottle of water with you in case you're not offered anything to drink during your interview.

>> **Use of technology:** This relates to virtual and phone interviews. Are you doing your interview via the Internet through a service like Skype or Google Hangouts? Find a quiet location where you can do your interview, preferably inside, where there is no noise from car horns, barking dogs, and the like. If your interview will include video, make sure you dress up as though you were going to a live interview. Also plan to have a nice background. For example, doing an interview with books or a nice wall in the background will give a good impression.

Initial screening interview

Initial interviews are usually done via phone or in person. Also referred to as *screening interviews,* these may last a few minutes or up to an hour. In general, if they last long it tends to be a good sign that you're doing well.

Initial interviews are usually conducted by a recruiter at the organization or someone in the human resources (HR) department. At a small employer, this interview may be conducted by the actual hiring manager or the person for whom you'd be working.

This is the first interview you'll have, and it's meant to screen out applicants to come up with a smaller set of candidates to send to the hiring manager. Most of the questions in these interviews will consist of verifying what's in your résumé and will be fact based to make sure you meet the basic requirements for the job.

On-campus interviews

These are another type of screening interview, but they're conducted on college and university campuses by visiting employers. These interviews may be done by someone in HR or by the hiring manager. On-campus interviews are typically more thorough in that the employer is looking to make sure you're a fit for the job or the organization so they can invite you to interview on site.

Most colleges and universities have on-campus recruiting software, managed by the career services office that allows you to sign up for *preselect interviews.* This is where you apply to interview with a certain number of employers. You then get notified if you've been invited to interview and you select an interview date and time. On-campus interviews tend to be competitive, especially when you're applying to a popular brand-name employer.

Interviewing with the hiring manager

When you've made it through the initial interview, your next conversation is typically with the hiring manager, who is the person you would be reporting to. This interview may include some of the same questions you were asked initially. But often, it's also a time for the hiring manager to get to know you, and vice versa, to get an idea of the potential working relationship. Here you may get factual questions, for example, pertaining to projects you did in school or previous jobs you've had. You may also get situational questions to get an idea of how you would react in specific circumstances. Here are some examples of situational questions:

>> Have you ever encountered an obstacle in trying to complete a project and if so, how did you resolve it?

>> Do you like working with customers?

>> Do you multitask? And if so, can you give me an example of where you've had to multitask?

>> Have you ever had difficult team members on a project and if so, how did you deal with them?

These are just a few possibilities out of the many possible questions you may be asked. The idea is to use your imagination to put yourself in those scenarios. Work on answering questions in a positive manner.

By the way, if you ever get asked whether you like working with customers or clients, the answer is always yes! But also ask the interviewer to elaborate on how you would work with clients or customers.

Interviewing with team members

You've made it far along in the process when you have interviews with your prospective peers. An offer is not yet guaranteed, but you can take it as a great sign that you've made it to this stage. You may meet with team members individually or as a group. These group meetings may seem intimidating, but remember to keep your cool and stay calm.

Some of the questions asked may be familiar ones from previous interviews and they can include factual and situational questions. Team members for the most part want to know you're qualified to work with them and that you can get along with them.

Sometimes, these team member interviews may be the hardest, and it's due to a few reasons. For one, employees may feel protective when a new member joins the team because they can take some of their work or responsibilities. As a result, you may get extra-hard questions. Do your best to answer these and keep a positive attitude.

TIP

Adding a new member to the team often changes the dynamic of a group, and people don't always like change. Don't let this scare you, and don't assume all team members will be this way. You may end up having great enjoyable interviews with your prospective co-workers.

REMEMBER

Becoming Familiar with Interview Platforms

With higher Internet speeds, better phone data plans and higher-quality video streaming, virtual interviews are becoming more prevalent. One or more of your interviews may be conducted via video or phone.

TIP

Here are some basic tips to make sure your conversation goes well with all these options:

>> **Find a quiet place.** Whether you're using Skype or doing a phone interview, make sure you find a quiet location where you won't be disturbed. If you're conducting a phone call, you can even lock yourself in your bathroom, if it's quiet. Don't do this if you're doing a video interview, though. If you're having a hard time finding a quiet space, contact your school's career center or your public library to see if they offer rooms where you can do your virtual interviews.

>> **Dress to impress.** Even with video interviews, you should dress like you would for an in-person interview. The person or people on the other end will most likely see you from the neck up, so in theory, you can wear pajama pants, but make sure you dress business casual from the waist up.

>> **Go wired instead of wireless.** If you're interviewing via phone, use a landline or a phone with a cord instead of your cellphone. This lowers the chance of your call getting dropped. If you have to do the call from your cellphone, use a wired earpiece or a wired headset instead of a wireless headset. Wires are bulky, but they tend to lead to better-quality calls.

>> **Use a computer instead of your phone.** Whenever possible, use your computer for a virtual interview instead of your phone. Computers tend to be more stable and provide better audio and video.

If you're doing a video interview via your laptop, try to connect it to the Internet via Ethernet cable instead of using Wi-Fi. Wireless Internet connections are not always reliable, especially if you're close to a microwave. Microwaves, when in use, tend to interfere with wireless Internet connections.

The goal here is to have the best possible conversation by leveraging the technology while also ensuring that it doesn't create distractions.

Interviewing via Skype

Skype is one of the most widely used applications around to communicate via phone or video. It works via the Internet, and you can download Skype for your iPhone, Android phone, or laptop or PC via www.skype.com. Skype tends to be reliable and high quality.

The application lets you make free audio and video calls if you're calling another Skype user. If you're calling a cellphone or landline, you'll need to buy some Skype credit to make those calls. Buy enough to last the entire duration of your call; $10 should be enough.

TIP

You'll need to create a Skype username if you don't already have one. Pick a name that is professional and even playful, as long as it's not offensive or unprofessional. Don't pick a name like PartyAnimal17 or something along those lines. A variation of your first initial and last name will work.

Now that you have a Skype username, you'll need to add the person with whom you'll be talking. Follow these steps:

1. **Open Skype.**

2. **On the left horizontal bar, click Contacts.**

3. **Add a new contact by clicking Add Contact under the Contacts menu or click the Add Contact icon at the upper right of your screen.**

4. **The interviewer will give you her Skype username or you can search for her.**

To initiate a call, select your newly added user. You have the option to start a video or an audio/phone call. Ask the interviewer if the call will include video or only audio. When in doubt, assume your call will be via video. This way, you can prepare by dressing appropriately and selecting a nice place for the background.

Interviewing via Google Hangouts

Google Hangouts are another popular way to meet online. If you have a Gmail or a Google account, you can easily join a hangout or create one. Most likely you'll receive a calendar invitation with a video link on the invitation, as shown in Figure 10-9. Conversely, you can create an invitation and add a video link to it.

To create a Google Hangout invitation:

1. **Open the Calendar application in your Gmail or on your phone.**

2. **Create a new event and add the relevant details.**

3. In the event details, next to Video call, click Add Video Call.

4. Save the event.

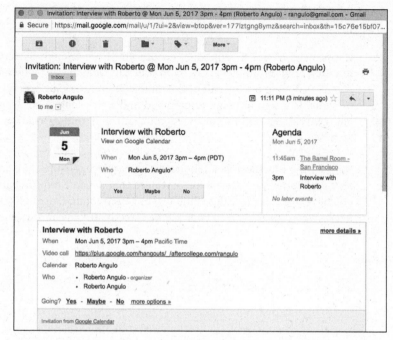

FIGURE 10-9: Accepting a Google Hangout invitation.

When it's time for your call, just click the video call link on your invitation. This will launch Google Hangouts on a new screen where you can turn video on or off. After you've made your choice, click Join. Similar to a Skype call, ask ahead of time if this will be a video or audio only call. And if in doubt, assume it will be a video call.

Using video conferencing

Video conferencing comes in many forms and is popular at large companies and universities. The good thing about video conferencing is that you don't have to do anything to set this up. All you need to do is show up for your interview. Most likely you'll be invited to go to a designated location at the employer's site or at your school, where the technology will already be configured.

REMEMBER

Dress appropriately, the same way you would for an in-person interview.

Interviewing via phone

Phone interviews are the most common, and this is how most initial screenings are conducted. Make sure you find a quiet area where there are no distractions to have your call. A landline phone is better because of the higher voice quality and lower chance of a call being dropped.

If you need to use a cellphone, ensure you have enough battery power for the duration of your call. Also plan to do your call from an area where you have a good signal. Dropping off the call in the middle of an interview because you lost power or signal is a sign of being unprepared and won't look good. Plan to have a fully charged battery before you have your call and find a location with a reliable signal.

When using Bluetooth headphones or an earpiece, ensure they have enough battery life. Better yet, use a wired earpiece that doesn't require batteries. This way you have one less piece of technology to worry about. Call quality tends to be even better when speaking into your phone directly. If you can skip the earpiece, do it.

» **Impressing the interviewers**

» **Being ready for tough questions**

» **Knowing what to do after the interview**

Chapter **11**

The Interview

The job interview is your chance to shine. Take advantage of your time with the employer to show that you're more than a set of skills and knowledge. Here you can highlight your personality, your aspirations, your thought process, and your passion for the job and for the organization. The interview is where you convince the employer that it needs to hire you.

Often, it's less about the message and more about the delivery. In this chapter, I fill you in on best practices for job interviews — from how to dress to what to ask — in order to gain an edge in your interview. I also explain what types of questions to anticipate. Finally, what you do after the interview is just as important as the interview itself. I offer tips on how to circle back with the interviewers in order to stand out.

You want to make a good impression, and this chapter helps you do exactly that.

Nailing Interview Etiquette

Regardless of the type of employer or culture, you should expect to follow some basic rules of conduct when going on an interview. The goal is to make a good mark and do it in a positive and respectful manner. You want the interviewer to not only appreciate what you would bring to the organization but also like you as a fellow human being.

Use the following guidelines to make a great impression.

Dressing the part

Your appearance is important, and any investment you make in dressing appropriately for your interview will pay off. Here are some tips to keep in mind:

After you've gotten a sense of how people who work at the company dress on a daily basis, follow these tips:

>> **Find out how employees at the organization dress, and then make sure you dress as well as they do or a little better.** This gives the impression that you'll fit in. It's also a sign of respect that you put in the effort to dress up for your interview.

You can find out how people dress in a few ways:

- Ask the interviewer ahead of time about how to dress for the interview.

- Ask friends who work at the organization.

- If you happen to be at the employer's location prior to the interview, pay attention to how people dress.

- Look on the employer's website or on Glassdoor to get a feel for what type of clothing people wear.

People may wear suits to work or they may dress business casual. If the environment is more laid back, they may even dress in jeans, or shorts and T-shirts.

If the dress code is shorts and T-shirts, you don't want to show up in a business suit; instead, wear shorts and a nice dress shirt. If the dress code is business casual, dress business casual; men can wear a sport coat (without a tie) and women can wear a pantsuit. If you're interviewing at a place where everyone wears a suit, make sure you wear a nice suit or dress.

>> **Wear clean, pressed clothes.** If you need to travel for an interview, pack two of everything in case you suffer an accidental coffee spill while on the road. Sure, you can explain that coffee or jam stain away during the interview, but not having to do that is even better. Iron your clothes and over-pack just in case.

Showing up to your interview well dressed and clean will make a positive impact. Conversely, showing up with a wrinkled dress or large stain on your shirt can make a less than-favorable-impression in the interviewer's mind.

>> **Opt for neutral colors, like black, blue, and gray.** If you're wearing a suit or dress, black or dark gray is a good neutral color. For men, light-colored dress shirts — either white or light blue — are the norm. Avoid wearing loud colors — they can distract the interviewer. Again, you want the focus to be on you as a person and what you bring to the organization, not what you're wearing.

>> **Tidy up your hair.** A clean and simple hairstyle is the norm at most employers, unless you're interviewing at a hair salon. If you're a guy, make sure to get a haircut if you think you need one. Do this a week or two prior and not the day of the interview; this gives your hair time to grow in case things don't go according to plan. Shave or trim any facial hair as well. If you're a woman, wear your hear conservatively and don't overdue it with an exotic hairstyle. Your hair is an important part of your appearance, but it shouldn't be the focal point or cause a distraction.

>> **Don't overdo cologne, perfume, and makeup.** You may be fond of a certain cologne or perfume, but try to avoid using it for your interviews. What you may think is a good scent may not be for the interviewer. You're better off being neutral. If you do decide to wear perfume or cologne, don't over do it. You don't want to leave a scent that overpowers the room or distracts from the conversation.

>> **Pay attention to your shoes.** Many people look at shoes, especially in business, to try to guess what kind of person you are. Make sure your shoes are clean or polished. They don't have to be brand new, but they shouldn't be worn out or too old. Wearing a good clean pair of shoes shows that you've put in the effort to present yourself well.

TIP

Avoid uncomfortable shoes or high heels. You may be taken on a tour of the organization, and you may have to walk long distances. Work on looking nice but also on being comfortable.

>> **Decide what to do about your tattoos and piercings.** Tattoos and body piercings are becoming more prevalent, but they aren't universally accepted. Some people find them offensive. Hide any tattoos or remove any body piercings that you can so that they don't become a distraction for the interviewer. On the other hand, if you don't want to work at a place where people get offended by tattoos or piercings, don't feel compelled to cover them up. If you end up not getting a job because of your tattoos or piercings, it may be for the best. Life is too short to be working with stuffy people.

>> **Avoid clothing or accessories that make political statements.** Unless you're interviewing at a grassroots organization or a political campaign, forgo wearing anything that makes a political statement. For example, a pin on your backpack that says "Free Tibet" shows support for a cause, but it may be one with which the interviewer may not agree. The purpose of the interview is to

establish a good professional and personal rapport. Talking about politics is risky because you don't know where the other person stands on certain issues. You're better off not approaching this subject in order to avoid a possible distraction that also has the potential to weaken the interviewer's perception of you. Even if the interviewer brings up politics, you can respond and make conversation, but work to bring the conversation back to the interview or to another topic.

TIP

Leave large pieces of jewelry, including big earrings and necklaces, at home. These can also create distractions.

Arriving early

One of the easiest things you can do to make a good impression is to get to your interview on time or early. By early, I mean 10 to 15 minutes, not more. Being punctual shows that you're prepared and that you're excited to be there. Conversely, if you're late for your interview, it shows that you may not care about it and that you don't have your act together. It can also be perceived as disrespect-ful. For example, if you arrive 10 minutes late and you're meeting with three people, you just wasted 30 minutes of other people's time. This is not a good way to start the interview.

REMEMBER

Plan ahead and show up early. A little punctuality goes a long way.

Here are some things you can do to ensure you get to your interview with plenty of time:

>> **Map the route.** Whether you're walking, driving, or taking public transporta-tion, go to Google Maps or use your phone to find out how long it will take to get to your interview. Add another 15 minutes to your estimate to give yourself plenty of time to get there.

>> **Check for traffic.** You can do this by using a map online and specifying the time you want to arrive. Or if you're driving, make sure to use your phone's GPS instead of your car's GPS, because your phone may have live traffic data, unlike your car.

>> **Stay close to your interview location.** If you're traveling to your interview and staying at a hotel the night before, stay close to where your interview will be the next day. If your interview is local, try to arrive at a nearby location — such as a coffee shop or a quiet place — early. That way, you can easily get to the interview on time.

>> **Don't make prior plans.** You have plenty on your plate the day of your interview. Don't plan any activities prior to it that may cause you to be late. If your interview starts midday or in the afternoon, leave the early part of the day open. Spend that time practicing or relaxing prior to your appointment. At the same time, your interview may go very well and the employer may ask you to stay and meet with more colleagues. If this happens, make sure you have the time to stay. Avoid scheduling any activities for an hour or two after your planned interview.

Getting rid of your chewing gum, food, and drinks

Chewing gum during an interview is a definite no-no. Throw away any chewing gum or snacks prior to your interview. If you have a cup of coffee, finish it or discard it as well. Your focus needs to be on the interview, not on your beverage. The only exception is water. Often, a glass or bottle of water comes in handy in case your mouth gets dry during the interview and you need to take a sip.

The interviewer may offer you something to drink prior to the interview. Accept the offer if you think you'll need some water. If offered coffee, pass on it, or take a cup only if the interviewer is also getting one and as long as it doesn't take too long to go get the coffee. You have limited time with the interviewer. A quick cup of coffee is fine, but don't spend 15 minutes going to the coffee machine for an espresso or a cappuccino. You can get one after you're done with the interview.

Handling lunch interviews

Lunch interviews are the exception where it's okay to eat during the interview. But follow some basic guidelines to ensure the interview goes well and that you make a good impression:

>> **Order simply.** Don't spend too much time looking at the menu. Make a choice quickly and be ready to order when the time comes. Your time is limited and you should focus on the conversation with your potential employer, so keep the time spent ordering to a minimum. Stick to an entree or a small plate instead of ordering a full-course meal.

>> **Keep it clean.** Don't order food that has the potential to create a mess — for example, sloppy joes or barbeque ribs. You don't want sauce running down your arm and on your sleeve or chili on your face.

>> **Eat lightly.** Plan to do more talking and less eating than the interviewer. Order a light plate or expect to not finish your meal. Stay focused on having a good conversation and don't worry about eating.

>> **Don't drink alcohol.** You want to be alert during the interview, so avoid drinking alcohol if you can help it. Don't have a drink, even if the interviewer has one. Order a soda or a lemonade instead.

Eliminating distractions

If you tend to get easily distracted, as I do, you need to do everything you can to stay focused. First, turn off your cellphone or put it in airplane mode before you get to your interview. You don't want your phone going off if you get a call or a text or any other notification. Also, avoid looking at your cellphone during the interview. Not only does it detract from the conversation, but checking your phone shows a lack of interest.

Try to sit facing away from a doorway or window. This way, you can stay focused on the conversation and not be distracted by people passing by in the hallway or by activity outside.

Making a Great Impression

The interview shouldn't be an interrogation. It's up to you to make it a two-way conversation between you and the interviewer. Don't worry. You can do this by staying alert and paying attention, knowing when to jump in and ask the right questions. Keep a positive attitude and stay confident. This will put you at the same level as the interviewer and allow you to put your best foot forward.

Starting a conversation

The key to making good conversation is to be a good listener. Expect to be on the receiving end of the questions, but remember that you'll also have the chance to ask questions. Take notes during the interview. Bring a nice pad of paper or notebook and a nice pen. Write down anything that jumps out where you either learn something or have a question about it.

When the opportunity arises, ask the interviewer to clarify if something was not clear. You can also ask for details about the job or the organization. This will shift the balance so the person interviewing you also has to answer questions, and this turns the interview into more of a discussion.

REMEMBER

Being nervous is okay. Interviewing is not easy. If all of a sudden you realize that you're having a conversation more than an interview, you're doing great. Give yourself a pat on the back.

Minding your body language

The key to good body language is to be as relaxed and comfortable as possible during your interview. Avoid sitting on your hands, crossing your arms tightly across your chest, or rocking back and forth on your chair. These are typical signs of being nervous or uncomfortable.

It's normal to be nervous. Sit comfortably on your chair or couch, but don't slouch or spread yourself on a sofa. Find a balance between not being too stiff and not being too relaxed.

TIP

In some cultures, it's bad manners to show the sole of your shoe to the other person. Avoid crossing your leg to prevent this from happening.

Making eye contact

A key to making a good impression is to establish a good rapport with the interviewer. One essential way to do this is to make eye contact. Yes, it's hard for many of us to look others in the eye, especially when they're staring right back. But this is an essential piece for communicating effectively. Making eye contact establishes a human connection with other people. It also lets you gauge their reactions as you talk and respond to questions.

You don't have to do this constantly. For example, I tend to stare off in the distance when I'm collecting my thoughts or when I'm giving a topic careful consideration. It's okay to look away. Besides, you don't want to be staring at the interviewer constantly. But when you're asking or responding to a question, you should look at the person.

When you make eye contact, you come off as being confident. This helps to make a good impression and will elevate you in the eyes of the interviewer.

TIP

If you have a hard time looking people in the eye, focus on an eyebrow or on the space between the person's eyes. This makes it easier on you and to the other person, it appears as though you're looking him or her right in the eyes.

Asking the right questions

The interview is about you, but you should expect to ask questions about the organization, the job, and its culture. An interview is an opportunity to get first-hand answers and to make sure the organization is the right place for you. By asking questions, you also show that you're enthusiastic about the organization and that you did your research.

In this section, I walk you through some questions you can ask. You most likely won't have time to ask all of these, so make a mental note of five or six questions you'd most like to ask. You'll also come up with more questions to ask as the interview progresses.

Potential questions to ask about the role:

>> What will the job entail and what will my responsibilities be?

>> Where does this position fit within the organization?

>> Is this a new position?

>> What would be your ideal candidate for this role?

>> How long do people stay in this job and what is the typical career progression?

>> Whom would I report to?

>> What would be your expectations for me in this role and what would be the measure of success?

>> Can I talk to other people currently in this role to get a better idea of what it entails?

>> What are some of the challenges associated with this job?

>> How do you measure and reward performance?

Organization culture is just as important as the role itself. Here are some questions you can ask:

>> Where do people usually have lunch?

>> Whom do you typically have lunch with?

>> Does the organization or do individuals participate in any after-work events?

>> When do people tend to get into work and when do they go home?

>> Do team members have any traditions or milestones that they celebrate?

>> How would you describe the culture here?

>> What do you like the most about working here?

>> What is one aspect about working here that you think could be improved?

Also ask specific questions about the organization based on your prior research. Your goal is to show that you prepared for the interview and that you're interested in working for the organization. Some thoughtful questions go a long way. Here are some questions you can ask:

>> I read your press release on _____ product or _____ partnership. How has this gone since the announcement?

>> I was looking at the company's stock price trend and saw that it's moving up. What's driving this growth?

>> What would you say is the most exciting project or one of the key initiatives that the organization is working on right now?

>> How is the organization leveraging _____ trend/technology?

>> Has the organization thought of expanding into this certain area or creating a product for _____?

>> What does the future look like for this organization?

These are just some ideas of what you can ask. If you're paying attention, you'll pick up on topics and come up with your own questions during the interview. Be thoughtful and learn from the answers you get. You'll learn more about the organization and the job while making a good impression in the process.

Avoiding the wrong questions

You may be asking yourself if there are questions you shouldn't ask during an interview. You're right to wonder about this. As the saying goes, there is no such thing as a dumb question. But during the interview there are questions you definitely shouldn't ask. Or at least delay asking them until you're about to get an offer.

Any question having to do with pay and benefits should wait until you've gotten an offer. An example of a question *not* to ask during your first interview is: "How much does the job pay?" This is a valid question and you need to know how much the job pays before you take an offer. But you still haven't gotten an offer. These questions are more about you than about the organization. At this stage in the process, it's better to leave these questions for later.

Here are other questions that are better left unasked for now:

>> How much vacation or paid time off do I get?

>> What benefits do you offer?

>> I have a DUI. Will you still hire me?

This last questions brings up an important point. We all have unique histories with parts that may be less than stellar. You should use your best judgment and be upfront with any information about yourself that you think needs to be shared. But do this after the interview and prior to accepting an offer or when asked.

WARNING

Avoid asking the interviewer questions about her family, partner, or political beliefs. Although those questions are interesting, they're not relevant to your interview. They'll create distractions and you could potentially end up in an uncomfortable conversation that could hurt your chances of getting the job.

Answering Difficult Interview Questions

Often, interviews are as much about putting you under pressure and seeing how you react as they are about the actual questions and answers themselves.

REMEMBER

Stay cool during your interview and keep calm. Be thoughtful and, most important, take your time in coming up with answers to the questions being asked. Avoid giving short, "canned" answers. The goal is to have a conversation and not make it an interrogation.

Talking about yourself

One of the most important things you'll get asked is to talk about yourself. It's ironic, but even though you're the expert on yourself, this could also be one of the hardest questions to answer.

A typical answer to the question may look like this:

I'm Roberto and I'm studying economics at Stanford University. I graduate in June and I'm looking to go into a business-related role at an Internet company.

This answer is fine, but it's too short and it doesn't convey a lot about you, what drives you, or your proposed contribution to the organization. You can add to your answer by saying something along these lines:

I'm Roberto and I'm studying economics at Stanford University. I'm really interested in sustainable businesses that create financial value and profit while also providing a benefit to society. I enjoy solving problems by coming up with creative solutions and look forward to applying my economics background in a technical field. I like what you're doing as an organization and strongly believe in your mission. I'd like to contribute to that mission by being part of your team.

Notice how the second answer conveys more passion and addresses a few points.

TIP

Come up with your own statement to describe yourself using this example as a guideline, making sure you cover the following points:

>> Factual information about your education

>> Your interest in the organization

>> What you bring to the organization

>> The research you've done on the organization

>> Your enthusiasm for joining the organization

You'll be surprised to find it's not that hard to come up with a great introductory overview. Practice it and commit it to memory.

Addressing your lack of experience

You're looking for your first job, and you have little or no experience. But most of the job openings you see advertised ask for some experience. Don't despair. Sometimes the business world doesn't make sense. Luckily, you can use some simple arguments and examples to prove that you do have experience. They didn't specify what kind of experience you need, right?

Most likely, you worked on projects at school, had an internship, or did some volunteer work. You can glean good examples of your experience from these activities.

>> **Internships:** Internships serve well to showcase your experience, particularly if your internships were in an industry relevant to the organization where you're interviewing or if the work is relevant to the job to which you applied. Make sure to highlight anything you did during your internship that is pertinent to the job. This can include a project you worked on, day-to-day work, or anything you did as part of a group.

» **Class projects:** Did you work on a course project with other students? If so, this provides an example of how you can work in a team. Teamwork is becoming more important these days. For example, if you worked on a marketing project to come up with a product launch plan, talk about this. If you worked on an engineering project to create a program, an app, or some device, talk about what the team did, how you worked with others, and the outcome of your work. This is real experience you can point to.

» **Student organizations and clubs:** Were you part of a student group, fraternity, or sorority? Were you an officer of the organization, in a leadership role, or part of an important initiative? Many organizations do fundraising for charities or for scholarships. Fraternities and sororities organize rush events to get new students to join. If you were involved in such initiatives, you can talk about your involvement and the outcomes — for example, how much money was raised, or how many new members were recruited to the organization. These are good experience points that have relevance in the working world and count as experience.

» **Coding competitions:** Showing experience is easier when you're applying for a software developer or data scientist role. One way to do this is through competitions. For example, on Kaggle (`www.kaggle.com`), you can participate in contests and rank yourself against other peers. You can point to your track record as a sign of how you can perform on the job.

» **Building a mobile app or website:** You can show off your programming chops and point to experience by building and launching a mobile app or website. Even if you build these on your own, without getting paid to do so, it shows that you have what it takes for the job. Even better, building something on your own not only shows experience, but also demonstrates that you take initiative.

» **Sports:** Your athletic career paints a great picture and can be leveraged as relevant experience. Being an athlete shows an employer that you have discipline, that you can work as part of a team, and most important, that you can achieve goals. Employers look for athletes particularly for sales-related roles, because sales jobs also require discipline and a focus on meeting a goal.

» **Sample writing:** If you're applying for a literary role, whether it's content writing, public relations, or copywriting, consider writing or pointing to pieces that you've written for public consumption. For example, you can write a blog using popular platforms like Medium or LinkedIn. If you've written for a particular publication or your school's newspapers, these are perfect samples that illustrate your writing experience.

» **Volunteer work:** Volunteer work is a great example of experience. It shows character because you've done the work for free, to help others. It also hints at what you're passionate about. Good examples of volunteer work include tutoring kids or teaching Sunday school. Organizing volunteers for fundraising events also count as great experience. Volunteering to make calls for political campaigns also counts if you're applying for a sales-related role.

>> **Part-time work and babysitting:** These activities are great for earning some spending money. Working in retail and dealing with customers point to your ability to be public facing, which is great experience to highlight. Babysitting hints that you have patience with children and that you're responsible; it also implies that you're trustworthy.

These are just some examples of experience that you can highlight in your interview or that you can build ahead of time. Think of other similar activities and plan your answer to this question accordingly.

Talking about why you're interested in the job

This is where your energy and enthusiasm need to come out. How you answer is as important as the answer. Talk about what you like about the role, the organization and where you see yourself in two to three years. Your vision for the future should align with the role you're seeking.

Here's an example of how you can answer if you're interviewing for a sales role:

> I really like talking to people and helping to address their needs. An inside sales role in your organization would allow me to do this. I like talking on the phone and getting bonuses, so this seems like the perfect opportunity for me to do what I like to do and to learn, while also delivering value to the organization.
>
> Your organization has a great sales training program. I look forward to helping grow revenue while growing as a sales professional.

I've underlined some parts in the preceding answer that relate to the sales job. Talking to people, addressing their needs, and delivering value are parts of your answer that directly tie your explanation back to the role. You can do this for any type of job.

Focusing on your accomplishments

This is a popular question among interviewers. You may get asked to name one of your biggest accomplishments or something that you're proud to have achieved. An example can include winning an award or a tournament.

An achievement can also be something that others may consider commonplace, but that may entail a bigger achievement for you. For example, being the first in your family to go to college or complete an advanced degree can be a big achievement.

Having a high GPA is a big achievement on its own. Doing it while also doing sports or working to pay for school is an even bigger achievement.

Did you do any fundraising that resulted in exceeding your goal? This is something you can talk about. Any volunteer work where you made an impact on people or on an outcome also counts as a good achievement.

Delving into setbacks and how you overcame them

Employers also want to know how you handle adversity or any obstacle that comes your way. Think of an example at school or from an internship where the odds were against you and you still came out ahead. You can also talk about failures and what they've taught you. Failures often teach us more than successes. For example, were you working on a team project and had team members drop off along the way? You can talk about how you and the rest of the remaining team members rallied to pick up the workload to complete your project on time.

Any setback relating to resource constraints is good to use because it directly relates to the working world. A good example could be how you worked with little or no resources to put on an event, such as a job fair for a student group or how you helped secured parts for a solar-powered car project, with little or no funding, and your team ended up winning a solar-powered car race.

I just made up these examples, but if they apply to you in real life, then you're a rock star! These are great experiences to mention.

TIP

Always stay positive and humble. When talking about challenges or adversity due to a person leaving your team or losing resources, spend more time talking about the team and how you collaborated. Be careful not to badmouth team members or to come off as being arrogant by saying you carried your team to achieving an objective.

Listing your top qualities

Employers normally ask this question directly, as in "Tell me about your top qualities." They may also ask this in a different way, such as "What would your friends or colleagues list as some of your top attributes?" You're probably an all-around great person with many good qualities, especially if you're reading this book. But for the purposes of the interview, think of some of your best qualities, either that you can identify or that your friends would point out, that an employer would find appealing.

Here is a list of good qualities with reasons why employers like them.

>> **Curious:** Curiosity shows that you want to learn. If you're eager to learn and improve yourself, this sends a good message to the employer.

>> **Focused:** Focus is the opposite of distraction. If you're focused, you're more likely to complete a task or achieve a goal.

>> **Committed:** This is a quality that in the face of difficulty or obstacles, keeps you on the path to completing an obstacle.

>> **Tenacious:** If you're tenacious, it means you don't give up. You keep trying until you reach your goal. This quality should not be confused with being stubborn, which can mean that you stay on a given course even though common sense and reason may tell you that you need to do something else.

>> **Disciplined:** Being disciplined means you follow the rules. Most employers like this.

>> **Organized:** Being organized can mean you're able to work well in a chaotic environment or able to put order where it's needed to get a job done.

>> **Dependable:** If you're dependable, it means team members can count on you to do your part on a project and deliver what you promised.

>> **Sense of humor:** I personally like this quality and think it's one of the best ones to have. A sense of humor allows you to get through tough times and defuse tense discussions or situations. If you have a good sense of humor that appeals to a wide variety of people, highlight this quality.

>> **Creative:** You don't need to be an artist to benefit from creativity. Creative people are good at solving problems, whether they relate to engineering, software development, life sciences, or any other field. If your classmates and friends describe you as being creative, definitely put this quality toward the top of your list.

>> **Thoughtful:** This can mean that you're kind and attentive to others. It can also mean that you're deliberate and careful in how you approach a task or a problem. The opposite would be that you're brash and rush into things.

These are just some of the many positive traits that make good potential employees stand out. Take stock of three to five of your top qualities and be ready to talk about them, giving specific examples.

TIP

Ask your friends, family, or significant other to name some of your top qualities, along with some examples. I sometimes find that others close to me tend to know me better than I know myself.

Acknowledging areas of improvement

Just as you're ready to highlight your virtues, be ready to talk about those less-than-virtuous qualities. Employers won't call them bad qualities. They'll most likely ask you to list some "areas of improvement." This is a tricky question. You don't want to say you have no areas to improve because that's simply not true — we can all improve in one area or another.

You want to show that you're self aware and know the areas where you need to improve. Don't make the mistake I made when I was interviewing for a job out of college. An interviewer at a large financial institution asked me about areas where my friends thought I could improve. I told her I didn't have any. That interview ended quickly and I didn't get the job. I thought I was being funny, but to the interviewer I came off as arrogant.

At the same time, you don't want to scare the employer away from hiring you. Think about areas where you can improve but make sure these are "noble" flaws. In other words, you want to give the employer an answer, but you also want these characteristics to be valued by the employer, even if you don't improve them. Here are some examples:

>> **Being too honest:** Honesty is a great virtue, but it can go both ways. In my case, for example, one of my best qualities is that I'm honest. But it's also one of my worst qualities. Sometimes I tend to be very direct with people and don't sugarcoat feedback. This honesty can come off as being abrasive. This is an area where I can improve, but also one that is okay if I don't improve.

>> **Working too much:** Having work–life balance is good and healthy, and working too much is not always a good thing. This is an area where I'm improving, but I still have a ways to go. If you're a workaholic, you can mention this as one of your weak areas. But rest assured, an employer won't be dissuaded from hiring you if you don't improve your work–life balance.

>> **Being too competitive:** If you're overly competitive and obsess about being the best or being in first place all the time, you may need to unwind and relax a bit. However, this is an example where an employer will still hire you, especially for a sales-related role, if you don't slow down in your competitiveness.

» **Taking loss personally:** It's good to keep your work and personal lives separate, especially when you suffer a defeat at work or in school. You can always go home to your friends and family for consolation. Taking work personally can be considered a flaw. But to an employer, this can be a good sign, because it shows you're passionate about your work, even if you take it too seriously.

TIP

Come up with your own list of areas where you can improve. Ask your classmates, friends, and family to help you identify them. Then pick the ones that you think an employer would find appealing and be ready to talk about those, using examples whenever possible.

Problem-solving during the interview

These are some of the toughest questions in the interview because they force you to think on your feet to come up with a solution.

Although this exercise may put pressure on you, it also gives you a chance to show off your critical-thinking, problem-solving skills, and your ability to collaborate.

REMEMBER

The interview is supposed to be conversational instead of being an interrogation. Bring the interviewer into the problem-solving exercise. Ask clarifying questions, write down any information you need, and make it a collaborative endeavor.

The key to doing well with these questions is to stay calm. Don't be your own worst enemy by letting your nerves get to you.

Problem-solving exercises come in many forms, but here are a few examples of what you can expect when interviewing for different kinds of positions:

» **Management consulting:** When interviewing at a management-consulting firm you may get asked something along these lines:

> A government-owned oil and gas company wants to build enough gas stations in the capital city so that drivers don't have to wait more than five minutes when stopping to get gas. How many gas stations do they need to build?

Some things you may ask want to ask about to set up the problem properly include the city's population, the percentage of people who drive, and the number of gas stations already in place. You may have to guess, or use your assumptions on the percentage of the population that drives, and on the time it takes to fill up. After you set up your variables, work on solving the problem.

- » **Patient care:** Healthcare-related job interviews usually include questions about patient care and are more situational. For example, if you're interviewing for a nursing job, you may hear the following:

  > You're doing the rounds checking on patients. As you enter a room, you find a patient unconscious. What do you do?

  This type of scenario may be less about being creative and more about remembering your training or specific medical protocol.

- » **Software programming:** Software-related interviews almost always have a coding component. You may get asked to look at some code and identify any errors or way to improve it. You may also get asked to build a specific routine to achieve a simple task. You may be given a database schema and be asked to create a SQL query to retrieve data. The possibilities are endless and too many to illustrate, but you get the idea.

- » **Customer facing:** Customer-facing roles are the most prevalent. Whether you're interviewing for a retail sales role, customer support, or food service, you can expect some situational questions. For example, you may be asked:

  > You're serving a table with a large number of guests and they're being lively. As you reach to give someone his beverage, another customer mistakenly hits your arm and you spill the beverage all over one of the guests. What do you do?

  Here you may ask about the restaurant's policy on giving discounts or free food in order to keep customers happy.

These sample questions give you a glimpse of what to expect during your interview.

TIP

With problem-solving and situational questions, stay calm, ask questions, and take notes when needed.

After the Interview

Congratulations! You made it through the interview. Whatever the outcome, you deserve some rest. Interviews can be exhausting, and you'll most likely be tired after even a one-hour interview. Take time to think about how your interview went and what you can improve next time. Practice makes perfect, and you'll most likely have more interviews, so learn from each one.

TIP

As your interview wraps up, ask the person for a business card or contact email so you can follow up with her. You can also ask your main contact for each person's email address. Alternatively, if you wrote down or remember the interviewer's name, you can connect with her and send a message via LinkedIn.

Following up

A good way to make an impression is to send a follow-up message to the interviewer. You can do this via mail, email, or LinkedIn if you don't have the person's contact information.

A simple thank-you message will do. If you come up with something you should have said during the interview or want to make a clarification, you can do this in your follow-up. It's not too late!

A nice note conveys to the interviewer that you're detail oriented and that you're interested in the job. It also helps you make a more lasting impression and stand out from other candidates.

Writing a thank-you note

Regardless of how the interview goes, send a thank-you note. Email is a good method for doing this. Although email is less formal than a printed note, it allows you to reach the interviewer immediately, and you're more likely to get a reply.

Your message should be short and positive and reference some point in the conversation. The following example shows a message to Lady Gaga, who you interviewed with for a kite surfer position at LGG Enterprises. You can be formal or informal in your email, depending on the rapport you've developed with the person.

> Subject: Thank you for your time
>
> Hello, Ms. Gaga.
>
> Thank you for taking the time today to talk to me about the kite surfer position at LGG Enterprises. I enjoyed our conversation and now have a better understanding of the role. Given the need to kite surf bigger and better waves, I'm excited about the prospect of being part of the LGG team to achieve or exceed this goal.
>
> During our conversation, you asked if I would be intimidated by surfing big waves. I wanted to clarify and add that with the right preparation and equipment, I am up for the challenge.

Please keep me in mind and if there is any question or concern I can answer, let me know.

Thank you again and best regards,

Roberto Angulo

Double-check your message for typos and make sure you spelled the person's name and the organization's name correctly. If the name is LGG, make sure you don't mistakenly write "Lgg." Spelling names correctly won't earn you points, but incorrectly spelled ones will give the impression that you lack attention to detail.

Checking on your status

After your interview, ask when you're likely to hear back about the position and find out who will get back to you. If you don't hear back or didn't ask, follow up with the employer ten days after your interview.

You can send a brief and simple email like this:

> Subject: Checking in: Kite surfer position
>
> Hello, Ms. Gaga.
>
> I remain very interested in the Kite Surfer position at LGG Enterprises and wanted to check if you're still looking to hire for the role.
>
> Sincerely,
>
> Roberto Angulo

If you're interviewing at more than one organization and an offer is imminent from the other employer, you can send a more forceful follow-up if you're interested in this employer, as shown here:

> Subject: Checking in: Kite surfer position
>
> Hello, Ms. Gaga.
>
> I remain very interested in the kite surfer position at LGG Enterprises and wanted to check if you're still looking to hire for the role.
>
> Since my interview, I've had conversations with another employer and it looks like that employer is close to making an offer. However, I would prefer to join the team at LGG Enterprises, so if I'm still in the running for the position, I hope you'll let me know.
>
> Sincerely,
>
> Roberto Angulo

Chapter **12**

The Offer

You have a job offer and now you have to make some choices. You really want this job, so do you accept the offer or do you ask for more? Or you have an offer and you're lukewarm on the organization, but you haven't yet gotten an offer from your preferred employer. Do you accept the first offer, decline it, or stall? In this chapter, I explain how to prioritize pay and benefits so you can make the best decision.

I also cover how to negotiate with an employer. Some employers have strict compensation guidelines in place, while others are more flexible. In either case, if you find that your offer is not comparable to market pay or to what your peers are earning, or if you have a better offer on the table, you can discuss this with the employer. The worst you can hear is "no." On the flip side, you may get a better offer.

Speaking of no's, you may have to go to a lot of interviews before you land that great job. Consider the journey a learning experience. In this chapter, I offer tips on how to build a professional network along the way.

Determining What's Important to You

Your first job is more than a paycheck. It's the start of your career where you begin to build your experience, your résumé, and where you start to create your professional network. You also get a better idea of what you want to do.

When looking at a job offer, look at the overall package and not just the money piece. Salary is definitely one of the most important pieces. You need to make a living wage in order to sustain yourself. But when it comes to asking for money above and beyond what you consider adequate, make sure you take the other components into account as well.

Salary

Salary is one of the main factors in evaluating an offer. You need to get paid well enough to cover your housing, meals, and monthly expenses. If money is your main motivator, then your goal is to take the offer that pays you the most. If you're starting as a full-time employee, your monthly or annual salary is the number to focus on. Full-time employment is also referred to as exempt employment. If you're exempt, you get a fixed salary and are exempt from minimum wage and any overtime pay.

On the other hand, you could be hired on as an hourly employee, or nonexempt.

REMEMBER

U.S. federal law — specifically, the Fair Labor Standards Act — requires that employers pay hourly nonexempt employees a minimum hourly wage. The act also requires employers to pay one and a half times your hourly wage for any hours worked above 40 hours per week.

Although this situation is less common, you can be hired as a contractor, where you get paid a monthly amount for a certain number of hours worked per month. Similar to hourly work, check to see what your hourly rate would be by taking the fixed amount you'll get paid by the number of hours you'll work. This number should meet or exceed the minimum federal hourly wage and be comparable to other offers you receive.

Taxes and withholding

As the saying goes, there is nothing more certain than death and taxes. And unfortunately, this is the case for taxes and your first job. Your new employer will deduct taxes from your pay, whether you're a full-time or part-time employee. So don't be surprised if your first paycheck is much smaller than what you originally expected. Some of the common taxes and deductions that get taken out of your paycheck include

>> **Federal income tax:** Your paycheck will include a deduction for federal taxes. This deduction will vary depending on how much money you make, your marital status, and the number of deductions you take.

>> **Social Security tax:** This tax funds the Social Security program, which starts paying out benefits when you retire. As of 2018, the tax is 6.2 percent of all earnings up to $128,700 in income. The employer pays another 6.2 percent for a total of 12.4 percent in Social Security tax. Note that if you get hired as a contractor, you may be considered self-employed. This means you'll need to pay the total 12.4 percent yourself. For example, if you make $100,000 a year and you're a hired as an employee, you pay 6.2 percent of your annual earnings in Social Security taxes, which is $6,200. If you're a contractor, you may have to pay 12.4 percent of your earnings, or $12,400.

>> **Medicare tax:** Similar to Social Security, you need to pay a Medicare tax. If you're an employee, the tax is 1.45 percent, and the employer pays another 1.45 percent. If you're a contractor, you need to pay the total 2.9 percent. Unlike Social Security, the Medicare tax is not capped at a certain income level. You pay this tax regardless of how much you make. In fact, depending on your marital status and whether you earn over a certain amount, you may pay a slightly higher Medicare tax.

>> **State income tax (depends on location):** Some states — like Alaska, Florida, Nevada, South Dakota, Texas, Washington, and Wyoming — have no income tax. Other states, like California, have some of the highest taxes. The amount of state tax depends on where you work.

>> **Other local taxes (depends on location):** Some cities and states also impose other taxes for state disability and unemployment insurance. And in certain states, you may have to pay a one-time *occupational privilege* charge that will come out of your first paycheck.

If you get hired as a contractor, you still need to pay taxes. You also need to pay the employer's share of federal income taxes and Social Security. So when you consider an offer that involves your being a contractor, take into account that you'll pay slightly more in taxes.

A brief guide to benefits

There's more to a job offer than salary. Some employers offer valuable perks that either help you create wealth or, depending on your circumstances, save you a lot of money:

>> **Relocation assistance:** In the rare case that you get offered a relocation, allowance, your employer may cover your moving and travel expenses. It may also give you an allowance to pay for housing while you find permanent housing. If your profession is in high demand, an employer may even give you money toward a down payment on a house. Some universities offer this perk to newly minted professors.

- ≫ **401(k) and matching:** Many employers, especially the larger ones, offer this benefit. A 401(k) allows you to save money from your paycheck before taxes get taken out. This is one of the few instances where you don't have to pay taxes on the money you make, as long as you save it in a 401(k) or comparable plan. The only catch is that the money needs to stay in the account until you retire. It gets better, some employers will match your savings contribution up to a certain amount. Ask about their 401(k) plan and their matching program.

   For more on 401(k) plans, check out Chapter 18.

- ≫ **Healthcare:** This benefit can be significant depending on your age, the number of dependents you have, and the type of coverage offered by your employer. For example, if you're still covered under your parents' insurance plan, coverage from your employer may not be that important. On the other hand, if you have significant healthcare expenses on a consistent basis — say, $200 a month or more on medical bills and medicine for yourself — the employer's plan may cover all these costs.

   Some employers cover all the employee's medical costs while others pay a piece and then ask participating employees to pay a portion of the monthly coverage. Ask the employer about specific healthcare benefits offered and how much you would need to pay to participate. Some employers also require you to wait 30 or more days after your start date before your health benefits kick in. Get clarification on this, too.

   TIP

   If you know you won't participate in the employer's medical plan because you already have coverage (don't go without coverage!), ask if the employer can substitute this with another benefit or slightly higher pay. Employers typically won't do such a substitution, but it doesn't hurt to ask.

   Most employers need to give you healthcare coverage if they offer it to all employees. So if you decline coverage initially and ask for it later, your employer is obliged to give you coverage.

- ≫ **Dental:** Employers often offer dental coverage as part of their healthcare coverage. Again, this can be a valuable benefit depending on your circumstances. If you have braces, intend to get them, or plan on having other orthodontic work done, this benefit can save you money. A sample plan may cover up to $1,250 in orthodontic services per year and then offer discounts of up to 50 percent or more on related services.

- ≫ **Vision:** Vision insurance tends to come with healthcare plans. If you wear glasses or contacts, this coverage can potentially mean a few hundred dollars a year in savings on glasses or contact lenses. Vision insurance is typically a lesser cash value bonus compared to dental insurance. But it's still a benefit worth considering.

>> **FSAs and HSAs:** Flexible spending accounts (FSAs) and health savings accounts (HSAs) allow you to save pretax money from your paycheck to cover health-related expenses. The benefit of opting in for one of these accounts is that it allows you to save from your pretax earnings. This lowers your taxable income and, depending on your tax bracket, can translate into substantial savings on certain expenses.

For example, if your tax rate is 30 percent and you contribute $2,000 into an FSA, you avoid paying taxes on the money you put into the FSA, so you save $600, which is calculated as follows:

$2,000 in annual FSA contribution × 30 percent tax rate = $600 in savings

Per IRS rules, you can contribute up to $3,450 for 2018 into a personal HSA or $6,900 into a family HSA. For FSAs, the annual limit is $2,650.

For more on FSAs and HSAs, check out Chapter 18.

TIP

>> **Gym and wellness allowance:** Yes, some employers offer this, and for those who do, amounts of $100 per month are not uncommon. You can get an additional $1,200 per year through this perk. Some employers offer onsite gyms. Although that's not the same as an allowance, an onsite gym allows you to save the cost of a membership, so it translates into a real savings.

>> **Commuter benefits:** Employers also tend to offer commuter spending accounts (CSAs) that you can use to pay for parking and public transportation to and from work. This benefit is similar to FSAs and HSAs in that you can contribute pretax dollars and lower your tax burden. The IRS sets limits on how much you can contribute based on your income.

>> **Company car:** This is a rare perk, but some organization may give you use of a company car if your job requires it or if you go to work in a place that requires you to have security and a driver. If your employer provides this benefit, it will save you a lot in not having to invest in transportation. Also, clarify whether you can use this benefit for personal use and not just for work.

Bonuses, commissions, and stock

Bonuses, commissions, and stock are other forms of compensation that are close to cash, albeit with a level of risk. The downside to bonuses and commission is that they are not guaranteed. But on the other hand, if you do exceptionally well in your job or the company does well, or both, then you can make a substantial amount of money.

Signing bonuses

Some employers may offer you a signing bonus to entice you to join the organization. This usually means you get a large cash payment on your first paycheck or toward the beginning of your employment. A signing bonus can come in handy if you're relocating for a job and you need to cover moving expenses.

WARNING

Signing bonuses usually require you to stay with the employer for some period of time. If you leave before that time, you may be required to pay back the bonus.

Bonuses

Cash bonuses can be tied to your job performance, the company's performance, or both. For example, if the company meets or beats revenue and profitability goals, then employees at a certain level may receive a bonus. In another example, if you work on the product or marketing side of the organization, you may get bonuses based on a successful product launch or its adoption or sales growth. Bonuses mean more cash in your pocket, but they can also move you to a higher income bracket, causing your tax rate to go up. In general, though, bonuses are a great thing.

TIP

Bonuses are structured in different ways. If bonuses are part of your offer, ask the employer how often bonuses are paid out and when have there been instances of bonuses not getting paid.

Commissions

Commissions are more common and usually the norm with sales-related jobs. Ask about commission structure details and also find out what percentage of employees earn commission, and how much on average. This will give you an idea of whether the commissions are attainable.

Stock

Stock options are common in startups and rarely do they result in a significant payout. You hear about early employees at companies like Google and Facebook becoming wealthy because they had stock options early on. Be wary, though. Stock options are not a substitute for wealth, and although they *can* result in significant wealth in some cases, they usually end up being worth little.

Restricted stock options (RSUs) are sometimes given at publicly traded companies. RSU structures vary across organizations, but in the most common cases, you get a certain number of shares for joining the company and then you vest a percentage over four to five years. For example, you join a company and you get 1,000 RSUs that vest over four years. The stock is worth $20 a share. So your RSUs in this case are worth $20,000. Because of the four-year vesting, you get 250 RSUs the first year, another 250 the second year, and so on until you vest all 1,000 RSUs. RSUs are almost like cash, but they carry some risk:

>> **You get them only if you remain with the company during the entire vesting period.**

>> **If the stock price drops to zero, the RSUs are worthless.** However, the risk of this happening is low. The stock price could fluctuate, though, to, say, $10 a share. But it can also go up, to $30 a share in this hypothetical example. So, your RSUs could end up being worth a lot more, too.

Experience

One of the most valuable aspects of your first job is the experience you'll get. The specific work-related knowledge you gain, the personal growth, and the know-how that you acquire as you work with others to solve problems and overcome obstacles will make you a more valuable employee. It will also strengthen your résumé and position you for better opportunities.

If you get an offer to work at a great organization, on a cutting-edge project or product, or with a great team in a key role that will make a big impact, consider forgoing some cash compensation if the offer is not high enough. A short-term cash sacrifice in exchange for investment in your professional development will lead to a great career down the line.

Flexibility and work–life balance

College students rank work–life balance and flexibility as the most important factors aside from salary when considering an employer. If you're of the same mindset and value flexibility, ask the employer about typical work schedules, vacation time, and its telecommuting policy.

For many people, better quality of life outweighs material wealth.

Company culture

It's not just about what you work on, but also whom you work with. If you work at an organization where the environment is cutthroat and people don't trust each other, is this worth more money for you? Or would you rather work at an organization where people work collaboratively and in teams, and the communication is direct and respectful?

A good work environment leads to productivity and happiness. For many, this also outweighs monetary compensation.

Employer brand

An employer's brand and reputation is also an important factor among first-time job seekers. Companies like Apple, Amazon, Facebook, and Google are among the best known employers. They also have good consumer brands. Working for one of these organizations looks great on a résumé and helps as a stepping stone for your next job. Although these employers tend to pay very well, consider the value of working for a popular employer and be willing to forgo some cash if needed.

Negotiating an Offer

It's natural to get excited when you get a job offer. It's a big deal! You may be eager to sign the offer and send it back right away. Don't do it, though. Hold onto it and give it some thought before you respond.

When you get a job offer, thank the employer. Ask when the company would like a response from you if it's not specified in your offer. If it wants a response immediately, ask if you can have at least a day to respond.

You want to stay calm and let the employer know that you're appreciative and interested. But you also don't want to appear too eager. Unless this is the absolute best job in the world, waiting lets you do the following:

>> **Allow other offers to come in.** If you're interviewing at other organizations — and you should — then this gives you time to evaluate other opportunities.

>> **Ponder what's important.** Evaluate your offer and determine if it's good for you. Think of the benefits being offered and if they're important to you. Also consider other benefits you'd like to have that are not included.

>> **Prepare questions.** Prepare questions to ask about your offer letter. You owe it to yourself to be familiar with everything that is being offered to you, including details on any bonus or stock, medical benefits, and other perks. Definitely get all these questions out of the way before you sign. The employer expects you to ask these questions, so don't feel awkward about it.

As soon as you get an offer from someone, reach out to other employers with whom you've interviewed and let them know. This usually makes them hurry to give you an offer if they intend to do so.

Dealing with an on-the-spot verbal offer

You may find yourself in a situation where an employer is giving you a verbal offer face to face or over the phone. You may love the offer and be tempted to accept it right then and there. Hold on a second!

I remember getting an internship offer right after my interview. My future boss offered me $18 an hour. That was a lot of money for me at the time, so when I heard the number, I was pleasantly stunned. My boss saw the look of shock in my face and said: "Okay, I'll make it $20 an hour." Silence is your friend. The lesson here is to hold tight for a few seconds or a minute before you answer.

Gaining leverage with multiple offers

Whether you are set on working for one organization or could care less, you should interview with three or more employers so you can get at least two offers. Having more than one offer in hand gives you leverage. It also lowers your risk of getting no offers at all.

Here are some ways you can use multiple offers to your advantage.

Speeding up an offer

An offer lets you tell another employer that you have an offer in hand and that it should move more quickly if it is still interested in you. You can do this via a simple email note as follows:

> Hello Ms. Gaga,
>
> Thank you again for taking the time to interview me. I remain interested in LGG but I also want to make you aware that I recently received an offer from another employer and I need to respond soon.
>
> Please let me know if you have any updates. I look forward to hearing from you.

A message as simple as this one will get the employer to either give you an offer or to tell you it has gone with someone else. That employer may also not respond. That's fine. Your goal is to have clarity one way or another so you can either get an offer or move on.

Getting more money

When you have two or more offers, it starts getting fun. You're in a great position to ask for a better package. Take a scenario where you want to work for Employer A, and it offers you $15 an hour. Then Employer B comes along and offers you $16 an hour. If you want to work for Employer B, and you believe you have a good offer in hand, you should take the offer from Employer B. If, on the other hand, you prefer Employer A, you can say something along these lines to Employer A:

> I'm excited about the prospect of working at Employer A. I've received another offer, though, and it proposes to pay me more. Employer A is where I'd like to work, but this other offer creates some hesitation. Is there a possibility to increase my compensation?

Here you can do two things:

>> You can tell Employer A what the other employer is offering and see if Employer A beats, matches, or comes close to the competing offer.

>> You can leave it vague and not specify what the other employer is offering.

The employer will either ask you what you're getting offered (it's okay to say) or will come back to you with a number, which may be more or less than the competing offer. There's no right strategy here. Do what feels right.

TIP

Be appreciative and humble when talking to the employer. You want to convey that you have another offer and that you're looking to make the best decision. But you also want to let the employer know that you value its offer, and that you're interested in working for it. You don't want to come off as playing both sides to get the best deal.

Researching salary information

Before you start negotiating, make sure you have a good idea of the market rate for someone in your role. Because it's your first job, keep in mind that it's an entry-level role.

One easy way to find out what you should get paid is to talk to people who have the same job. Do you know someone with the same role at another organization or someone at the organization? Do you have a close enough relationship to ask such individuals how much they make and for them to share this information? If you do, then definitely ask.

PayScale is another great resource for salary data. You can look up average pay for your role and similar ones, at your experience levell, and narrow it down to your location. Just go to www.payscale.com, click Get Free Salary Report, and choose Job Offer. Then answer a series of questions, and you get a high-level compensation report. If your offer consists of an hourly rate, PayScale will convert it to an annual salary.

Negotiating other perks besides money

Even when you make the case for getting a higher salary, the employer may not have the flexibility to bump it. Some employers have rigid pay guidelines where each position belongs to a certain pay grade. As you get promoted or change roles, you can move to a higher pay grade. In other cases the employer just may not have the budget to increase your offer. Instead of cash, you can ask for other perks:

>> **Vacation:** Vacation time is often referred to as *paid time off* (PTO). Your offer letter should include mention of vacation and holidays. If the organization offers two weeks standard of PTO, you can ask for an extra week or more of PTO instead. This can be a valuable perk if you plan on traveling or taking a medical leave. Your employer may offer additional time off for medical reasons. If you plan on taking such a leave, discuss it with the employer.

In business jargon, five days of PTO mean the same as a week of PTO (five workdays in a week) or 40 hours of PTO (40 work hours in a week).

REMEMBER

>> **Later start date:** Unless you're joining a company with a preset start date for a specific training program, you may be able to ask for a deferred start date. If you're just graduating from college, you deserve at least a few weeks off. Take some rest and extend your start date if you can.

>> **Working from home:** Also referred to as *telecommuting*. Some jobs are able to be done from home. Because this is your first job, you should maximize your time at work so you can learn as much as you can and get to know your colleagues. Nothing beats face-to-face collaboration. Still, it may be nice to work from home one day a week or once every other week. If this is something that appeals to you, you can ask for this type of flexibility.

Accepting an Offer

When you and the employer agree on your compensation and package, the next step is to for the employer to send you a formal offer letter. The offer will usually include a signature line for you to complete. The employer will ask you to either email or mail back the signed offer letter, or bring it with you on your first day of work.

Get excited and show your enthusiasm to the employer! Sign the offer letter and send it in as soon as you can. After you've sent it, check in with the employer to make sure the company got it.

TIP

Employers almost always send formal offer letters. If you get a verbal offer but nothing in writing, insist on a letter or email. Be wary of any employer that refuses to put an offer in writing.

Sample offer letter

Here is a sample offer letter for a marketing coordinator role at LGG, Inc. This is a full-time job with a base salary of $60,000. Your actual letter may include more details on benefits and any bonuses you're being offered.

Re: Offer of Employment with LGG, Inc.

Dear Roberto:

On behalf of LGG, Inc. (the "Company"), I am pleased to offer you the position of marketing coordinator at the Company, reporting to me, Lady Gaga, Big Chief at LLG, Inc. In this position, you will be expected to devote your full business time, attention, and energies to the performance of your duties with the Company. The effective date of your new role will be _____.

The terms of this offer of employment are as follows:

Compensation. The Company will pay a base salary of $60,000 annually, payable in accordance with the Company's standard payroll policies, including compliance with applicable withholding. The first and last payment by the Company to you will be adjusted, if necessary, to reflect a commencement or termination date other than the first or last working day of a pay period.

Benefits. You will be entitled, during the term of your employment, to the Company's standard paid time off (PTO) policy, which is currently ten days of PTO per year, accrued at a rate of ten hours per month — in addition to paid holidays and benefits covering employees at your level, as such may be in effect from time to time.

Immigration Laws. For purposes of federal immigration laws, you will be required to provide to the Company documentary evidence of your identity and eligibility for employment in the United States. Such documentation must be provided within three business days of the effective date of your employment, or your employment relationship with the Company may be terminated.

Employee Proprietary Information Agreement. As a condition of accepting this offer of employment, you will be required to complete, sign, and return the Company's standard form of Employee Proprietary Information Agreement.

General. This offer letter and the Employee Proprietary Information Agreement, when signed by you, set forth the terms of your employment with the Company and supersede any and all prior representations and agreements, whether written or oral. This agreement can only be amended in a writing signed by you and an officer of the Company. Any waiver of a right under this agreement must be in writing. This agreement will be governed by New York law.

I look forward to your joining the Company. If the forgoing terms are agreeable, please indicate your acceptance by signing this letter in the space provided below and returning it to me, along with your completed and signed Employee Proprietary Information Agreement.

AGREED AND ACCEPTED:

By: _____   Sincerely,

Name: _____   LGG, Inc.

Date: _____   By: _____

Name: Lady Gaga, Date

Big Chief

Declining an Offer

If you decide to decline an offer, either because you accepted another opportunity or because you don't like the offer, let the employer down gracefully. Be humble and respectful, thank the employer for her time, and do your best to explain why you're declining the offer.

The best way to turn down an employer is to do it over the phone. It's more personal and warmer than doing it via email. It's also harder, but often doing the right thing is hard. Here's one way you can let the employer know that you're turning down her offer:

First of all, I'd like to thank you for the consideration you've given me and for the time you've taken to talk to me about [NAME OF ORGANIZATION] and the [JOB TITLE] role.

I've decided to accept an opportunity at [NAME OF OTHER ORGANIZATION].

This was a hard decision, but the role I'm taking aligns well with my goals. Thank you again for interviewing me.

TIP

Customize your message based on your situation. If you don't have another job offer lined up, remove any mention of another role or employer. Even better, wait until you have at least one other offer before you turn one down. You don't want to be left without any job offers.

WARNING

Don't burn bridges when declining a job offer. Do it in a good way and politely. People often move to different organizations, companies get bought and sold, and you may later change your mind and discover you want something different. You could end up working with someone down the line at an organization you turned down.

Although it's better to turn down an offer over the phone, you should also follow up with an email. Keep it positive and appreciative.

> Subject: Thank you
>
> Hello [NAME OF CONTACT PERSON],
>
> Thank you for considering me for the [JOB TITLE] role at [NAME OF ORGANIZATION].
>
> Although I am not joining your team, I enjoyed meeting with you and the rest of the group and look forward to staying in touch.
>
> Sincerely,

TIP

Think back on any good conversations you had with the people who interviewed you. These are individuals worth connecting with on LinkedIn. Being connected is a good way for them to remember you. And you never know . . . they may have other roles in the future that may be of interest to you. For more on adding LinkedIn connections, check out Chapter 15.

Dealing with Rejection

You don't always win them all, and when interviewing, you're bound to get turned down by some employers. This is normal, particularly in competitive fields where there are more candidates than jobs available. Here are some ways to deal with the potential disappointment:

>> **Diversify.** In other words, pursue more than one opportunity and don't just focus on one. If you pursue only one job, you'll be disappointed if you don't get it. On the other hand, if you interview at a number of organizations for jobs you like, one loss will be offset by one or more wins.

>> **Don't take it personally.** Employers are often busy and may interview dozens of candidates for a particular role. Employers are looking for the best fit between a candidate and the job and look at your skills, experience, and education. If you aren't chosen for a particular role, it's not because of who you are as a person. It has to do with your particular skills at the time of your interview.

>> **Learn from the experience.** Take each interview as an opportunity to improve. For example, you'll find yourself getting less and less nervous as you talk to more employers. You'll also get an idea of what questions to expect and you'll get better at answering them. Take this as an opportunity to identify gaps in your skills or knowledge where you can brush up and be ready for future interviews.

>> **Connect with the employer.** Invite the interviewer to connect with you on LinkedIn and thank that interviewer for his time. He may not have a role for you now, but may have one for you in the future.

>> **Take a break.** Are you doing a lot of interviews and starting to burn out? Take the weekend to relax and not think about your job search. This helps lower your stress levels and also helps you do better in the future.

Replying by email

Always respond to employers, even if they're giving you bad news. It's good form to take the high ground and respond positively. An email is good enough in this case. Here's an example of a note you can send:

Subject: Thank you

Hello [NAME OF CONTACT PERSON],

Thank you for getting back to me in regards to the [JOB TITLE] role at [NAME OF ORGANIZATION]. Although I'm disappointed not to have received an invitation to join your team, I appreciate your time and attention.

Please keep me in mind for future roles. I look forward to staying in touch.

Sincerely,

REMEMBER

A closed door now can always open in the future. Keep good relations with employers who turn you down — they may have a job for you down the line.

Getting feedback on why you didn't get the job

After you reply to employers, try to get them on the phone to see if you can get feedback on why they turned you down. Some employers will hesitate to do this, either because they get busy or because they may find it awkward to talk to you after they've declined you for a role. Some companies may be unable to provide feedback because of internal policies.

Good employers, though, will give you insight on what you can improve or where there were gaps in your candidacy. These employers know to invest in a candidate pipeline, and they should welcome you back in the future once you've addressed any concerns. Here are some ideas on how you can state your question to the employer or start the conversation:

>> Thank you again for considering me. Do you have any insights on how I can improve if I were to apply again to your organization?

>> Thank you for your time and attention. Could I ask you for any insights on how my candidacy stacked up compared to other candidates for this role?

TIP

Employers are more likely to give you feedback over the phone than in writing. Call employers for feedback instead of asking them over email.

Chapter **13**

Relocating for the Right Job

Your dream job may be in another city or in another country. If you have little or no commitments tying you down to your current location then it makes it easier to pursue opportunities, wherever they may be.

Before you jump in and accept an offer, though, take time to research what it costs to live there. If you've already jumped in and accepted an offer without doing your research, well, that's okay. It's never too late. Your high-paying job offer may all of a sudden not look as good if it's in an expensive city like New York or San Francisco. These cities are notoriously high priced, where even if you make six figures, you need to find roommates to live comfortably. On the flip side, if your job is in a city like Tucson or Minneapolis, you may be able to rent or more easily buy a two-story house with a swimming pool and tennis court.

Do you like going out and meeting people or eating at good restaurants? In this chapter, you learn how to figure out the scene at the cities you're considering.

Evaluating the Cost of Living

The cost of living, and more specifically the cost of housing has a big impact on how much of your take-home pay you're able to enjoy. Some basic research will help you get a good idea of how far your pay will go in the city where you'll end up living.

The San Francisco bay area, for example, is among the most expensive in the country. The area is a hub for tech innovation and it attracts talent from all over the world. This, in turn, drives up housing prices. It doesn't help that San Francisco is surrounded by water, so it has little room to build more housing. Salt Lake City is an up-and-coming technology hub. But unlike San Francisco, it is surrounded by plenty of land, so it leaves plenty of room to build housing. This helps to keep the cost of real estate down.

Depending on your preferences, you can determine the right job and location for you by comparing various locations.

Calculating cost of living on PayScale

PayScale has a great tool called the Cost of Living Calculator in which you can enter your job title, salary, and two locations. The site will give you the equivalent salary you need to make at each location in order to have the same standard of living. Just go to www.payscale.com/cost-of-living-calculator to check it out.

TIP

The report not only shows you the cost of living differential, but it also breaks it down by housing, utilities, groceries, and transportation. You can print or download this PayScale report to negotiate higher compensation from an employer if you think your offer is low. For more on negotiating salary, turn to Chapter 12.

Researching cost of living on NerdWallet

NerdWallet is a great site for financial advice, and it also has its own cost-of-living calculator that gives you a good second opinion. NerdWallet doesn't have as many cities as PayScale, but it gives you a more detailed cost-of-living report, showing actual median rent prices, median home prices, and the comparable price of random but useful items like a six-pack of beer and a carton of eggs.

To use the NerdWallet cost-of-living calculator, go to www.nerdwallet.com/cost-of-living-calculator.

Deciding Where to Live

Most people starting out tend to rent instead of buy, so in this section, I assume you're renting. Plus, it's also good practice to rent first and then buy when moving to a new location. This gives you an opportunity to check out your new city and its surroundings before settling down. When you're ready to buy, check out *Home Buying Kit For Dummies* by Eric Tyson and Ray Brown (Wiley).

TIP

Here are some things to take into account when looking for an apartment:

>> **Proximity to work:** Living close to work is important if you intend to spend a lot of time there and need to be in or out by certain hours. It also reduces your commuting costs.

>> **Access to public transportation:** In some cities, you're better off taking public transportation than driving. If this is the case for you, consider finding a place near a bus or subway line that leaves you close to work.

>> **Restaurants and activities:** This may or may not matter to you, but living within walking distance or a short drive of restaurants, grocery shopping, or stores usually carries a premium in terms of price. Keep this in mind when looking for a place.

>> **Gym and pool:** Apartments often have community swimming pools and a gym. These benefits are included in your monthly rent. This is a bonus if you like to work out or swim.

>> **Schools:** If you have kids, you'll want to look for an apartment in areas with good schools.

TIP

Many employers, especially larger ones, tend to have lists of areas where it's good to live. Others have employee listservs or Facebook groups where you can ask for housing recommendations. In some cases, employers may even have negotiated rates with housing and apartment management companies. Ask your prospective employer to point you in the right direction.

Finding out how walkable your city is with Walk Score

Walk Score (www.walkscore.com) is a great site and app to figure out how good a location is in terms of being able to get to work or other locations by walking, biking, and taking public transportation.

Enter your prospective job location on the site or a place where you're considering living, and Walk Score will return a walk score, bike score, and transit score for the specific location. The site will display maps showing how far you can get around by walking, by riding your bike, and by taking public transportation. Walk Score also shows you a map with a crime rating, showing where there are higher incidents of personal crime and property theft. It even includes apartment listings.

This handy site gives you a quick snapshot of prospective living locations.

Finding an apartment on Craigslist

Craigslist often comes up as one of the top ways to look for housing. The site hasn't changed much since it launched more than 20 years ago. It has a simple design, yet it also contains a wealth of information from people who post listings for house and room rentals. Craigslist also has powerful filters to narrow your search.

To use Craigslist, just go to www.craigslist.org. The site allows you to filter by radius, number of bedrooms and bathrooms, type of housing, and other aspects. You can browse through the results on a map or as a list.

TIP

Anyone on the Internet can post a housing listing on Craigslist for free. Use your spidey sense, and if a potential landlord or roommate seems shady, bring a friend with you to look at the place. Also avoid sending money to people over the Internet unless you're sure they're legit.

Finding housing on Apartments.com

Apartments.com is another site worthy of your attention. It's dedicated to housing and it claims that its research team has visited and photographed more than 400,000 properties nationwide. The site tends to have more corporate apartment listings as opposed to individual apartment listings like Craigslist. Listings on Apartments.com have detailed pictures to give you a good idea of what each property is like. The site includes a phone number for you to call about a listing. You can also email property managers through the site.

To find apartment listings, just go to www.apartments.com.

Letting your Facebook friends know you're looking for a place to live

If housing is too expensive, you can also share an apartment or house with roommates. This tends to be cheaper. Plus, you get more house for your dollar by pooling resources. The question is how to look for roommates.

One of the most reliable ways to connect with potential roommates is to find them through people you know. Facebook is a good way to do this.

You can announce that you're looking for roommates by posting on Facebook. (You probably want to set the privacy of the post so just your friends see it, instead of the whole world.)

TIP

You can also post to specific groups on Facebook. If you belong to any private groups related to student organizations or classes, post to those as well.

Tapping into alumni networks

Do you belong to a fraternity, sorority, or another social group? Do they have private Facebook groups or email lists? If so, these are good places to let people know that you're looking for roommates or housing.

To ensure you get the best response possible to your post, include the following information:

>> Where you'll be working

>> When you graduated and what you majored in

>> The start date of when you need a roommate and for how long

By including all this information, you put more data points out there to help get people's attention. Your post may get forwarded to others, too, so the more detail you include, the more likely you are to get a response.

TIP

Many colleges have local alumni groups throughout the country. Ask your alumni association if it knows of any local with whom it can put you in contact.

Making Sure You Have Things to Do

Moving to a new city can be daunting. The more you research it ahead of time and find things to do, the better you'll adapt once you get there.

Luckily you can find a number of resources to learn about activities, landmarks, nightlife, and restaurants.

Meeting like-minded people through Meetup

Meetup (www.meetup.com) is a social networking site and app centered on local events. Sign up for free and join groups that are interesting to you. The site has more than 280,000 groups focused on hobbies, sports, politics, and other interests in more than 182 countries. You'll get updates on things to do in your city or town, and you'll meet people at these events.

Turning to TripAdvisor

TripAdvisor is a great resource for finding out about attractions, landmarks, outdoor activities, and shopping. Sure, it's mainly geared toward tourists, but when you're new in town, and you're looking for fun things to do, it's a great place to start. If you don't end up finding things to keep you busy, you'll at least know where to take friends and family when they come to visit you.

To use TripAdvisor, just go to www.tripadvisor.com, click Things to Do, and enter your city. You can filter by categories such as museums, outdoor activities (like hiking or golf), and nightlife.

Discovering entertainment on Thrillist

Thrillist is a newer service and currently lists 40 major cities in the United States. Use it to get ideas of things to do in or around town and to find out about local events, bars, and restaurants. Whereas TripAdvisor gives you landmarks and attractions, Thrillist is more dynamic and showcases activities and events that are happening now. You can visit the site often to get news on coming activities. Just go to www.thrillist.com.

Finding food on Yelp

If you're into eating out, Yelp will give you an idea of what kind of restaurants are in the area. This is great service for finding local restaurants in any category. It lets you drill down by neighborhood and you can narrow by price range and sort by reviews. Just go to www.yelp.com.

Getting Around a New City

If you're moving to a rural area or a very expansive city, you'll most likely need to drive to your job, unless you end up living close to work. Ask the employer or your new co-workers how they commute. In densely populated cities like Washington, D.C., New York, and San Francisco, many people take public transportation to work. In cities like Phoenix and Miami, for example, where the distances are long and the heat is intense, it's easier and probably cooler — both figuratively and literally — to drive.

Public transportation

Taking public transportation is your best option when commuting into downtown in a large city. These cities tend to be congested and, unless your employer offers parking, you may have to pay $30 or more a day to park downtown. Luckily, cities like Boston, New York, D.C., and San Francisco have great public transportation. You can take either buses, light rail, or metro lines to work. If you look at the major cities in Europe and Asia, the public transportation tends to be even better.

An easy way to find out your best route to work — whether you're using public transit or not — is to use Google Maps. But you already knew that. Another option is an app called Citymapper, which, as of this writing, works for Baltimore, Boston, Chicago, Los Angeles, Montréal, New York, Philadelphia, San Francisco, Seattle, Toronto, Vancouver, Washington, D.C., and a slew of cities around the world. The public transit department for the city you live in might have a trip-planning website or app, too.

Car sharing

Do you like to drive but don't really need a car for work? What if you only need to drive on occasion to get away on the weekends or go grocery shopping once a week? One option is car sharing.

With car-sharing services, you pay an annual or monthly fee and then an hourly rate every time you rent a car. The advantage of these services is that you can pick up a car from one of many convenient locations and rent by the hour.

Here are some of the popular car-sharing services:

>> **Zipcar** (www.zipcar.com): Zipcar is one of the largest services in the United States. You can pay for a car by the hour. It has locations throughout the United States where you can pick up cars. The only caveat is that you need to return your car at the same location where you picked it up.

>> **Enterprise CarShare** (www.enterprisecarshare.com): You pay an annual membership fee and then an hourly or daily rate depending on how long you use a car.

>> **Getaround** (www.getaround.com): This service works the same way as the others, except you rent cars from other people instead of renting them from a company. You can get cars by the hour or by the day.

Carpooling

You're probably familiar with ride services like Lyft and Uber. Both offer carpooling services that allow you to share a ride with others when going certain places. You can take advantage of carpooling through each of these apps. If you're commuting along a common route every day, you're very likely to find these services to be cheap and fast.

Lyft calls its carpooling service Lyft Line, and you can select it from your app by choosing the Line option. Find out more at www.lyft.com/line. Uber's carpooling service is called uberPOOL, and you can select it using the Pool option in the app. Learn more about it at www.uber.com/ride/uberpool.

Once you start your job, talk to your co-workers and see if they want to carpool with you. If you don't have a car of your own, you can pitch in for gas money and they'll make some spare cash giving you a lift to work. Win-win!

5

Starting Your First Job

Make the most of your first job by taking advantage of every opportunity to learn.

Adjust your career path as you receive feedback from mentors and as you discover interesting jobs that others do in the organization.

Grow your professional network in order to be more productive and expand your future possibilities.

Know when to mix business relationships and friendships and when to keep them separate.

Chapter **14**

Learning as Much as Possible from Your Job

Your first job is more than a paycheck. It's a chance to acquire new skills and knowledge. Don't sweat it, it's not like going back to school. It's more of an opportunity to learn while you work. The more you learn, the more you can contribute. And the more you can contribute, the better your chances of getting promoted within the organization or moving to other roles at another employer.

If you're a shy person, this is the time to come out of your shell and meet other colleagues. You have an opportunity to learn from your team members, people in other groups, and your superiors. Be curious about what they do and how they do it. Compare notes. Sit in on meetings and listen. You don't need to participate.

Does your employer offer any training or learning opportunities? Take advantage of these. Examples of training include productivity classes or programs on how to learn sales techniques. They also include trips to conferences on the latest technology as it relates to your field. Over time, you'll become the go-to person for members of your team on certain topics.

Setting Up Check-Ins with Your Boss

Depending on your job or internship, you will have a supervisor, a mentor, or both. Your supervisor is your boss and the person you report to. She's the one you talk to about pay, vacation, and your performance. In some cases, you may have a different person who is assigned to be your mentor. For example, in an internship, your mentor is someone on your team who is more senior, but not your boss. This individual is there to show you how things work, to help you navigate and find what you need within the organization, and to acquaint you with the company culture. In a software development or coding internship, you may report to an engineering manager or director, but you may be assigned to work with a technical lead who will work with you on projects, oversee your assignments, and even review your code.

Checking in with your manager is important for a couple of reasons:

>> It's a chance to update your manager on your progress.

>> It's a chance to get feedback on your contributions to the group and on how you're doing.

Managers often have more than one direct report. Plus, they have their own work to do. This means they may not always have the chance to check in with you. By taking the lead to give your manager periodic updates, you're helping your manager out.

Periodic check-ins come in many forms, like the following:

>> **Weekly check-ins:** These are also referred to as *one-on-ones* and are the most common. At a minimum, you should have a weekly meeting with your manager — even if it's for 15 minutes — to give her an update on what you're doing and to get any feedback on your work. Look at these meetings as a chance to get constructive feedback that will help you improve.

TIP

Keep a running list of items you want to discuss with your manager during your one-on-one. This will help you make the most of this valuable time and prevent you from drawing a blank during the meeting.

>> **Daily standups:** In engineering, these are also referred to as *daily scrums*. These tend to be brief team meetings where everyone gets a turn to give a quick update on what he or she is working on for the day and to cover progress since the last update.

TIP

Don't show off and never be afraid to say you don't know something. This is your first job. You're not expected to know everything. You'll impress your colleagues more by admitting you need help, learning, and growing as a valuable contributor to the team.

>> **Quarterly reviews:** Many employers have quarterly reviews, especially in corporate settings. These meetings happen with your manager where you establish goals for yourself for the upcoming or current quarter and review your goal progress from the previous quarter. These goals can include completing certain projects or deliverables. They can also include training or performing a certain task, even if not tied to a goal.

>> **Annual reviews:** These meetings are the same as quarterly reviews, but as the name implies, they happen once a year. Pay raises may accompany these annual reviews.

TIP

You can accomplish a lot in a quarter or a year, and often it's hard to remember what you did. Take notes of your work as you go so you can have a good update for your manager.

Being Proactive and Taking on Projects

A good way to learn is by joining projects where you can work with others. If you get an opportunity to be part of an initiative, take it. For example, is your company launching a new product or service? You can contribute to the effort by testing the product or by joining the sales team that will be involved in its launch. Or for instance, if the organization is adopting a new tool or software for a business function, such as new customer relationship management (CRM) software, you can be part of the team that gets trained on the software, works on the integration, and trains others.

Some of the advantages of being proactive and volunteering for projects include the following:

>> **Learning:** You always have the opportunity to learn, whether it's from a team member or from the training that comes with implementing new tools, software, or processes.

>> **Getting your name out:** When you work on projects, especially those made up of people from other parts of the organization, you're making yourself known. This gives you an advantage, because your name may come up for consideration more often when it comes to new roles, projects, or promotions.

> » **Making connections:** Another advantage of working on groups made up of people from other parts of the organization is that you meet people in other departments who can help you with your job down the line. For example, if you work in sales and form part of a group that includes engineers, you can later call on them to ask engineering-related questions.

TIP

If you're in a field that involves programing, design, or writing, you can volunteer to review other people's work. This helps the other person while also giving you ideas on how you can improve your own work.

You may ask what the disadvantages are. You typically won't get paid more for taking on extra work, and you still have to do your own job. But the gains in recognition, knowledge, and new relationships make up for this.

Knowing What Others Do on Your Team

As the saying goes, you learn something new every day. One way to make sure you keep learning is to make an effort to find out what others do in your organization. This exposes you to new jobs you may not have known about.

Be curious. If you're wondering what someone in your organization does, ask him. Other questions you can ask include the following:

» How did you get to where you are?

» How long have you been doing your job?

» Do you like what you do?

As a result, you may get the idea to explore other career paths. If you're in sales, you may like being a sales engineer. If you're a writer, maybe you'll find out that you can do content marketing. And if you're in client support, you may learn about a human resources role that interests you.

Taking Advantage of Learning Opportunities

Most employers offer formal channels for you to acquire new knowledge and skills. You can often take advantage of these opportunities during work hours. As long as the things you want to learn relate to your job, your employer should be supportive.

Going to lunch-and-learns

These are typically held weekly and during lunch and tend to be more common at technology startup companies. Typically, these organizations encourage employees to share knowledge with others. Topics can be about anything, including the following:

>> **What someone does in her job:** This can include accounting, customer service, sales, or programming.

>> **How to use a specific tool or piece of software:** This can include how to do certain things in Microsoft Word or Excel, for example, or how to create PowerPoint presentations.

>> **Group updates:** A manager or the president of the company may give an update every Friday on how the business is doing and any new developments. These events are good ways to stay up to date on what's going on in your organization.

In some cases, the employer sponsors lunch or drinks. In other instances, everyone brings his or her own food. Either way, this is a good use of your time. If your employer organizes these types of sessions, make it a point to attend.

Subscribing to email lists

Organizations often have internal email lists, organized around topics such as new product releases, product ideas, and idea contributions, where employees can subscribe to receive announcements and to engage in internal discussions around certain subjects.

At AfterCollege, for example, we use Google Groups to manage email distribution lists around various subjects. Anyone in the organization can subscribe to updates on topics ranging from new engineering releases to sales-related announcements and even updates on employee benefits such as 401(k)s.

TIP

With a lot of these tools, you can often customize how frequently you get emails. You can choose to get them in real time, at the end of the day, or once a week. Choose the frequency that's right for you.

The advantage to joining these groups, even if you don't contribute to them, is that you get exposed to communications around topics of interest, giving you yet another opportunity to learn.

Joining online collaboration groups

Collaboration tools are similar to lists, but they have more chat and messaging functionality and they're more interactive. Examples of internal collaboration tools include Slack and Chatter (by Salesforce). With Slack, you can join a group depending on the policy set by the owner of the group.

If your organization uses these tools or similar ones, you can join and be part of the conversation or you can just observe. You can join groups related to engineering, sales, marketing, and other topics. These are good learning media because you get to witness discussions by experts in your area of interest.

Taking advantage of tuition reimbursement

Most employers encourage you to take advantage of learning opportunities, and many of them offer tuition reimbursement on courses that relate to your work.

Some large employers like Apple and AT&T offer up to $5,000 in tuition reimbursement. If you're pursuing an undergraduate degree, employers can reimburse up to $25,000 in tuition in some cases. Even if the reimbursement is minimal — say, $100 per year — you should take advantage of it.

Typically you may need to meet certain requirements in order to get reimbursed:

>> **Employment type:** You may need to be a full-time employee in order to get tuition reimbursement.

>> **Length of employment:** In some cases, you may need to be employed for a certain amount of time — for example, six months — before you can qualify for this benefit.

>> **Relevance to your work:** It's common for employers to reimburse education-related expenses only if they pertain to your work or if they allow you to advance to another role within the organization.

>> **Course grade:** Your employer may also require that you get a minimum grade for a course, such as a B or a C, in order to get reimbursed. If this is the case, make sure you can do well in the course before signing up for it.

Learning through online courses

If your employer doesn't offer tuition reimbursement, don't despair. You can take advantage of free or inexpensive online courses through services like Coursera, Skillshare, and Lynda, which allow you to browse and search for available courses. For example, if your job requires that you work with numbers and that you do a lot of analysis, you may decide to take a course on Excel and spreadsheets in order to do your job better. You can often audit these courses for free and pay to get teaching materials, grades, and a certification. At a minimum, your employer should be willing to give you time to take online classes that are relevant to your job. Your employer may even reimburse you for part of the course fee or the entire course fee if the subject matter ties directly to your work.

TIP

Justifying time to study to your employer should be simple. The more relevant skills you acquire, the better you become at your job and the more productive you'll be.

For more learning resources, check out Chapter 17.

Participating in training

Employers often offer ongoing training opportunities. These can be recurring or single events where an outside trainer comes in to talk about a topic. Examples of these include the following:

>> **Sales techniques:** Whether you're in sales or not, this can be invaluable training because it can include how to better listen, how to do a needs analysis for a client, and how to close a contract.

>> **Team building:** Some organizations take a group of employees on obstacle courses or on daylong workshops where you solve fun problems with others. These events may seem playful, but they really show you how to get along with others in a group in order to achieve a common goal.

>> **Negotiating skills:** If you interact with clients, suppliers, or others in your group where you need to negotiate contracts, access to resources, or timelines, this sort of training can be invaluable.

>> **Project management:** Your employer may send you to special project management training where you learn how to coordinate projects and plan out timelines, resources, and ensure goals get achieved.

>> **New software:** If your organization is adopting a new piece of software or tool to help improve or automate a process, this is usually accompanied by some training. If this new software applies to your job and you have a chance to participate in training, make sure to sign up.

>> **New devices or procedures:** If you work in a medical setting or hospital, depending on your job, you can learn about new procedures or devices that relate to patient care. The medical field is always evolving, and it behooves you to stay ahead of any trends that come about.

>> **Teaching techniques:** Teachers often have the opportunity to go to workshops to learn about new teaching techniques and learn from veteran educators.

If you're lucky enough to have training at work, take advantage of it. You never know, but when it comes time for a promotion or getting a highly coveted role in an organization, what can set you apart from others is that little extra piece of knowledge or training you completed.

IN THIS CHAPTER

» **Breaking bread with your co-workers**

» **Getting together with your colleagues in a group**

» **Reaching out to colleagues on other teams**

» **Treating your clients as colleagues**

» **Staying in touch with colleagues online**

Chapter **15**

Building Your Professional Network

The people you meet and the connections you make in your first job will stay with you for years. You'll most likely make good friends at work. You also have the chance to develop a professional network of people who can help you secure your next job or promotion. They can make you aware of new opportunities and, as they move to other organizations, they can recommend you to their employers. These folks can also be your best references. And you'll be able to help *them* down the line, too.

If you're outgoing and make friends easily, networking will come naturally to you. If you're shy or socially awkward, don't worry! The tactics described in this chapter are easy to follow, even for someone who'd rather connect with his computer than a human being.

REMEMBER

Ultimately, if you do a good job and you're a good person, people will want to work with you now and in the future. This chapter is about how to nurture your professional relationships with these people.

Having Lunch with Your Colleagues

This advice may seem stupid or simple, but it's pretty powerful! You can work with someone for an entire day, but you may not get to know her as easily until you spend some more relaxed time with her. Lunch is a perfect opportunity to get to know colleagues in a more informal setting.

You'll probably be taken out to lunch on your first day of work. If you're starting a job as part of a cohort of new hires, you'll definitely go out with others to lunch. In many cases, though, it may feel like your first day of school, and it may take a week or two to get into the rhythm of having lunch with your co-workers. Make the most of these opportunities to develop a rapport with your colleagues. You don't need to become best friends, but you want to have good relationships with others on your team.

REMEMBER

Good relationships create trust, and trust helps with work, especially if your work involves working as part of a team.

Participating in Group Activities

Participating in group activities is a great way to build rapport with your co-workers. These activities can be employer-sponsored or things you organize on your own with a small group of colleagues. The types of events come in different shapes and sizes. Some are planned; others improvised. They can include the following:

>> **Going out for drinks:** It's not uncommon for co-workers to go to a nearby bar or restaurant for a beer after work. Just make sure you don't drink too much. Drinking with your co-workers is different from drinking with your college friends. If you start feeling a little buzzed, switch to Coke.

>> **Jogging or walking:** Does your work have walking paths nearby? Going for a walk or a run with a colleague is a good way to socialize. You can make it a 15-minute walk for an afternoon break or a long run after work. You can also substitute meetings where you're sitting down with walking meetings outside. You can still talk business, but the change of atmosphere can help strengthen work relationships.

>> **Playing sports:** Your employer may participate in sports activities, such as a bowling, softball, or soccer league. If so, these are great ways to get to know co-workers in a fun and mildly competitive way. Sporting events also expose

you to people across the organization who you may not normally work with. Plus, you get the chance to meet with higher-ups in the organization.

>> **Scavenger hunts:** We do these at my company from time to time and find that people come in refreshed and excited the next day. New relationships are forged and people are more at ease when they come in to work.

>> **Volunteer projects:** Some employers organize volunteer events for employees to attend. These can include feeding the homeless, packing lunches, or painting a school. Not only are these activities good for society, but they're also good opportunities for you to interact with your colleagues.

>> **Skydiving:** Okay, so this activity is a bit extreme and not all that common. And you definitely won't find many employers sponsoring skydiving events. But at my first job, one of the vice presidents and my manager organized a weekend skydiving trip, unofficial and not company sponsored. Anyone who wanted to participate could go. People from across the organization went, and it really brought people together. I decided to skip it, though. I'm not too fond of heights, so going on runs or out for drinks was enough for me!

All these interactions help you make personal connections with others at work, and they help strengthen your professional relationships. Keeping your work life and personal life separate is a good idea, but we're all human, and getting to know the people you work with is never a bad idea. You may end up getting valuable advice on how to do your job better, or you may get connected to someone on another team with a job within the organization that may interest you.

REMEMBER

Don't feel obligated to attend a social activity if you don't feel comfortable. Skydiving isn't for everyone. But don't let yourself off the hook entirely — socializing is hard for some people, so if you can't find *any* social activity that you feel comfortable with, challenge yourself to try at least one.

Collaborating with People on Other Teams

Your ability to work with others across the organization depends on the type of job you have. If you work in a field such as sales, help desk support, finance, engineering, or marketing, you most likely have the opportunity to work with people in other groups. Your goal here is to make meaningful contributions that will be noticed by others.

Here are some ways to ensure that your contributions will be noticed if you happen to be in one of these roles:

>> **IT or help desk support:** If your job is to support others within the organization, you can make a good impression by going above and beyond to provide guidance and following up. If you don't know the answer to a question, make it a point to research the answer, do your best to find a solution, and follow up with the colleague in need. In a support role, even if you don't know the answer, it's up to you to help get that answer. Employees who go above and beyond tend to be rewarded.

>> **Sales engineering:** If you work in a technical role at a sales-driven organization, you may at some point be called upon to help answer technical questions during a sales call. Salespeople love to have engineers at meetings because it helps them put solutions together for clients. These meetings are great opportunities for you to make a name for yourself with the sales organization, while also contributing to solutions that clients will appreciate.

>> **Finance and accounting:** Finance and accounting jobs can include managing accounts payable, managing accounts receivable, and doing financial analysis and reporting. Regardless of the type of finance you work in, these functions touch most parts of an organization, which means you can make significant contributions. For starters, being detailed oriented and helping others with finance-related tasks such as expense reimbursements can earn you kudos. If you're lucky enough to be in a position to present some form of financial analysis to management, you can give a great presentation and answer questions — making your worth known in the process.

>> **Human resources (HR):** Roles in this field can range from recruiting to helping employees understand benefits. People in HR often go unrecognized and are sometimes even vilified because employees tend to deal with HR only when they have problems. If your first job is in HR, you can excel by helping others do their job better. Help employees with their benefits or help recruit the best talent to the organization. You'll start earning the respect of co-workers and build your network.

>> **Project manager or coordinator:** Project managers are in charge of ensuring that everyone is aligned on a project. They're usually responsible for communicating progress. You can volunteer to be the one to give updates to other groups on your team's progress. Even if you're a junior coordinator, you may be doing a favor for someone more senior by taking some of the load off him when it comes to giving progress reports to other teams.

Keep others updated on what you and your team are working on, but don't show off or take credit for other people's work. People appreciate getting updates and being educated, but nobody likes a showoff.

Viewing Your Customers and Clients as Colleagues

Clients are an important part of your professional network, too. They see the results of your labor. So, do a good job for them, work with them to complete their projects well and on time, and you'll earn fans for your entire career.

TIP

Some common practices that clients appreciate include the following:

>> **Giving status updates:** Clients appreciate frequent updates — at least weekly — on work that you're doing for them. If you have metrics or any other data you can share with your client, prepare a nice report and do it frequently. You can give these updates via email or phone, but in person is even better!

>> **Being a champion:** If you work for a large organization and serve as the point of contact for your client, be your client's champion within your company. Clients appreciate having someone at the organization who can work on their behalf and help them cut through bureaucracy and navigate to get what they need.

>> **Getting answers:** Clients may ask questions to which you don't have the answer. Unless your organization has policies that say you need to transfer the person to someone else, do your best to get them an answer and help them avoid the hassle of having to figure it out on their own.

REMEMBER

Clients appreciate good service. If you can get them to see you more as a colleague or partner and less as a vendor, they'll start asking for you more — and that's a *good* thing! If they move to another organization, they can seek you out to help their new employer. They can even ask you to come work for them! You can grow your professional network and expand the number of opportunities available to you by going above and beyond for your clients.

Maintaining Your Network Online

As you've probably figured out by now, social networks are a great way to stay in touch with people. But they aren't just for keeping up with your friends and family. You can use them to maintain your professional network, too.

LinkedIn is a great tool for keeping track of your work contacts. People often make the mistake of seeing LinkedIn as a way to grow their networks. But LinkedIn is more of a way to keep track of the network that you've already built, or are building, through your work and school relationships. It's a visual representation of the connections with people that you already have in place. Still, it's an important tool because it makes it easy for you to keep track of colleagues as they change jobs and get promotions. It also allows you to update others as you progress in your career. And if you ever lose their contact information, you can get in touch with them via LinkedIn.

Although LinkedIn is the traditional way of staying in touch with professional colleagues, more and more people are connecting with co-workers on Facebook.

Friending trusted co-workers on Facebook is okay. But when you cross that line and accept friend requests from colleagues, you need to make sure your co-workers don't see any incriminating pictures or updates that may affect your reputation at work.

WARNING

When it comes to your boss or someone at a higher level, you're better off not connecting on Facebook. You don't want your boss knowing about the awesome three-day weekend you took if you neglected to turn in an assignment on Friday. You also don't want them to see how you were partying the night before, even if you come to work on time and get your work done.

If you get a friend request from someone at work, you can do one of three things:

>> **Ignore it.** You can simply ignore the request and hope that the person doesn't ask you about it. This approach usually works well.

>> **Accept it.** You can accept the connection knowing that your co-workers will know anything personal you post on Facebook from that point on.

>> **Accept it, with limits.** You can create friend lists on Facebook so that you limit what certain groups of people see. For example, you might want to create a friend list called "Business" or "Professional," and assign all your co-workers and clients to that list; that way, you can accept friend requests from business contacts but filter what updates they see.

WARNING

Lately, Facebook has become a place where people share and comment on their political views. Unless you work for a political organization (like the Republican Party or MoveOn.Org), you should avoid discussing politics at work. If you're sharing your political views on Facebook, you may inadvertently offend a co-worker. Keep this in mind when friending co-workers or when filtering updates and comments through friend lists.

TIP

Check out Chapter 7 for more on how to clean up your social presence and create friend lists.

6
The Part of Tens

Check out useful sites and job boards, each with its own unique job-relatad data and search features, to help you find the job that's right for you.

Continue learning using popular online resources so you can be more productive at work and to advance in your career.

Learn some of the key vocabulary you need and get familiar with concepts like flex spending accounts in order to understand your benefits and negotiate a good job offer.

Chapter **16**

Ten Sites for Finding Your First Job

Searching for a job is easy. Finding the one that's right for you can be hard. Fortunately, you have access to dozens of tools and job boards where you can look for jobs and internships. Even better, you can have sites recommend jobs to you and email you as they find new ones.

In this chapter, you learn about some of the best sites to help you find your first job. Some of them stand out because of the size of their jobs database. Others are good resources because they cater to first-time job seekers. Some of these sites have sophisticated algorithms baked in to guide you in determining what careers and jobs are better suited for you based on your field of study and preferences.

Here is an introduction to what these sites offer you as a first-time job seeker.

Indeed

Indeed (www.indeed.com) is the largest job site on the Internet. It crawls the job sections of company websites and takes jobs from other job boards, making it an aggregator of jobs from other job sites as well as from direct employers.

Because of this, I tell job seekers that if they know what kind of job they're looking for, they should start with Indeed.

Using Indeed is simple. Start by entering a job title and a location. You can enter a city or a zip code. You can even enter **remote** as a location and it shows relevant jobs. When you get the results, you can narrow them by experience level, job type, and location.

Indeed gives you an option to sign up for email alerts that send you updates on jobs matching your search. This feature comes in handy; you can unsubscribe at any time. The sheer volume of jobs on Indeed makes it a site worth using.

AfterCollege

AfterCollege (www.aftercollege.com) is geared exclusively for college students looking for part-time jobs and internships and for soon-to-be and recent graduates looking for their first job. It solves an issue that affects most first-time job seekers: not knowing what jobs and organizations to apply to. The site makes you aware of relevant jobs you didn't know were out there by giving you recommendations based on your educational background. It also takes your feedback when using its Explore tool to improve its recommendations.

TIP

For a detailed overview on using AfterCollege's Explore tool to get personalized job and internship recommendations, turn to Chapter 3.

Another way AfterCollege matches you with jobs is by letting employers target opportunities to students based on what school they attend and, more specifically, by major and student group affiliation.

Go to www.aftercollege.com/career-networks and type in your college or university name. You'll be presented with a list of academic programs and students groups for which AfterCollege has created career networks. These career networks contain curated jobs for students at a particular group or academic program.

Most of the opportunities are entry-level. Register on AfterCollege to get jobs emailed to you based on your school and major. These emails will also contain Explore recommendations. And if you opt in, you can get emails from employers visiting your campus or wanting to connect with students with your educational background.

LinkUp

LinkUp (www.linkup.com) is similar to Indeed in that it crawls the job sections of employer websites. It has fewer jobs, but the jobs it has are higher quality because they come exclusively from employer websites and not from other job boards or third parties. In other words, it has one of the "purest" jobs databases in the market. When you apply to a job via LinkUp, you're taken back to the employer's website.

LinkUp is basic and simple to use, but don't let appearances fool you. Its job index is updated daily, and it includes more than 3 million unique jobs. You can do a search by keyword and location like most other sites. Click the Advanced Search link to do a more granular query using keyword and predefined job tags like "intern/new graduate."

LinkedIn

LinkedIn (www.linkedin.com) is the top online professional network. Although it's geared more toward midcareer professionals and people in industry, it does offer tools that will help you find your first job.

For starters, create a profile on LinkedIn so people looking for you online can easily find you. When people look you up online, your LinkedIn profile tends to come up near the top. As you meet people during your job search, LinkedIn is a great way for you to connect with them. You can also include a link to your LinkedIn profile on your résumé.

TIP

To learn more about creating a LinkedIn profile, check out Chapter 7.

LinkedIn has other useful features. One of them is asking for recommendations from classmates and colleagues, and showing these recommendations on your profile. You can also follow employers and get notified when new opportunities are posted. LinkedIn also lets you see where alumni from your school work, so you can get an idea of what the usual career path is for someone graduating from your alma mater. These features are covered in more depth throughout this book.

University or College Career Centers

Your university or college career center will usually have its own job board. This site can be a valuable resource because it contains jobs and internships from local employers looking to hire students and graduates from your school. Each school's job board varies in functionality.

Most of these sites aren't great when it comes to functionality (they often look like they were built 20 years ago), but the thing to focus on here is the content. Career centers usually allow employers to post jobs for free. This means you get some smaller employers posting that normally would not post.

Go to your university career center's website and look for a "students" section, a section labeled "job search," or a prompt for students to log in.

REMEMBER

Most career center job sites require you to create an account. You should sign up in order to access exclusive jobs and to get notifications of on-campus visits and other notable events.

AngelList

If you want to work at a startup, you need to check out AngelList (www.angel.co). The site started as a marketplace connecting startups with investors and now has a job board with more than 68,000 jobs from 24,000 startups as of 2017. AngelList puts a lot of information about startups in one place, including team members, funding events, and most important, product information.

When evaluating a startup, product information and the investment it has received are two important aspects to consider. AngelList makes it easy to see this data, along with jobs.

Glassdoor

Glassdoor (www.glassdoor.com) is simple to use and is also one of the larger job boards. What makes this site unique, though, is the reviews from employees and ex-employees who give feedback on what it's like to work at the various organizations. Use Glassdoor to find jobs of interest or look up employee reviews for employers you've found on other sites.

Glassdoor has a simple-to-use interface. When you're looking at the details of a job, you can easily toggle between the job detail, company overview, and most important, the employee reviews on the organization.

TIP

For a deeper dive on how to gauge employer morale on Glassdoor, take a look at Chapter 4.

Craigslist

Craigslist (www.craigslist.org) is the largest classifieds site on the Internet and has a presence in 57,000 cities across 70 countries, according to Wikipedia. This is a valuable resource for finding jobs because of its local focus. Although the opportunities are not necessarily entry-level, you'll find jobs from local businesses large and small.

The site is simple in design and hasn't changed much since 1995, but don't let the design fool you. Craigslist has a lot of postings on a city-by-city basis. And an advantage of its simple design is that you can easily use the site from your mobile device.

Internships.com

As the name implies, Internships.com (www.internships.com) is dedicated to helping you find an internship and lists more than 192,000 of them. Like most sites, it lets you search by keyword and location. But when you get to the search results, it provides some nice filtering options that are specific to internships. For example, you can filter by paid or unpaid internships. Another filter lets you segment out the type of employers — whether nonprofits, companies, or government agencies.

Association Websites

Are you a member of a student group on campus? If so, most of these groups are affiliated with a state association or a nationwide organization that usually has its own job site. Here you can find entry-level jobs and internships from employers looking to reach members of your group.

Examples of national associations include the Society of Women Engineers (SWE; http://societyofwomenengineers.swe.org). The Florida Nursing Students Association (FNSA; www.fnsa.net) is an example of a statewide group, with individual on-campus chapters. These groups also tend to have job sites. Find the national and state associations for your field, and look for job listings there.

The value of these association job sites comes from the fact that they list opportunities from employers interested in individuals with your affiliation and skill sets.

WARNING

Job sites are not impervious to scams. Be cautious of job listings that ask you to send money or share bank account information or other sensitive data such as your Social Security number. Never share this information or send money, no matter how good an opportunity sounds!

Chapter **17**

Ten Places to Gain Skills and Become More Employable

Never stop learning. The more skills you have, the higher your chances of getting the job you want.

I remember getting ready to graduate with my economics degree. I landed my first full-time job at BBN, a pioneering company that invented the Internet and early technology like email and the modem. I had taught myself HMTL and knew about databases, and this ultimately helped me get the job.

Luckily, you now have dozens of resources at your disposal to learn new skills. Some of these tools are free, and others are not. But the great thing about all of them is that you can access most of them easily online. You can also get certified on what you learned in a matter of weeks.

Here you get a glimpse of ten of these resources.

TIP

Keep track of courses you take and skills you acquire by adding them to your résumé or profile.

Coursera

Coursera (www.coursera.com) is one of the largest providers of online courses. It boasts over 2,000 courses, offered by top instructors at some of the best colleges and universities.

You can take courses on subjects such as business analytics and search engine optimization (SEO). The courses run for four to six weeks and cost $29 to $99 each. You earn a certificate after you complete the course.

You can also do a specialization, which takes you deeper into a specific topic through projects and assignments. Specializations typically consist of four to ten courses and run for four to six months. You can specialize in popular topics such as game design and development, software programming, and data science.

You can even get a master's degree on Coursera, which takes anywhere from one to three years. Coursera gives you the flexibility to earn your degree online, from top universities. The cost can be up to $25,000. If you're considering getting an online degree, weigh the benefits of the online degree to your career before making this type of commitment. The specialization may be a good start.

Udemy

Udemy (www.udemy.com) is similar to Coursera in that it offers online courses. In fact, it has more than 55,000 courses, making it one of the largest services. The two main differences are that Udemy courses are not necessarily backed by universities, and they do not lead to a degree or certification.

Udemy is more of an open platform, where any expert can create a course and offer it either for free or for a fee.

It's great for brushing up on things like using Microsoft Excel or any other skill that will help you do your job better.

TIP

Are you an expert in a certain area? Consider putting together a Udemy course to share your knowledge. It looks good on your résumé and will impress potential employers.

Lynda.com

Lynda.com (www.lynda.com) is another service that allows you to learn new skills. It offers almost 6,000 courses. You get the usual selection of tutorials on how to program and how to use tools such as Excel and PowerPoint. But Lynda also has more business-oriented tutorials on how to be a better worker and colleague. For example, it offers a course on how to be assertive.

The site offers a free 30-day trial. After the trial, you can pay $19.99 a month to get full access to all Lynda courses. For $29.99 a month, you can view courses offline and download course materials.

TIP

Before you pay for any of these learning resources, check with your school, your local library, or your new employer to see if they have a subscription you can use.

Khan Academy

Khan Academy (www.khanacademy.org) offers coursers in core subject areas such as history, economics, geometry, electrical engineering, geometry, chemistry, and physics. The site is free and relies on donations to run its operations.

The site is geared more toward students from kindergarten through high school than adults. Still, the site is useful because it allows you to get a refresher on basic concepts that can relate to your everyday work.

Khan Academy also offers free test-prep courses, including one for the NCLEX-RN, which graduating nurses need to take before they can start working.

Codecademy

Codecademy (www.codeacademy.com) focuses specifically on teaching people how to program. The site offers interactive courses on how to code in 12 different programming languages, including popular ones like Python, PHP, JavaScript, and SQL.

If you're looking to go into a more technical discipline that involves coding, this service is worth a look to give you an idea if programming is right for you.

Udacity

Udacity (www.udacity.com) offers free stand-alone courses and also has study programs, for a fee, which it calls "nanodegrees." One of the good things about Udacity is that it focuses its programs on fields that are in high demand by employers. Nanodegrees have specific start dates and the cost starts at a few hundred dollars.

The service focuses on creating pathways to well-paying careers. It collaborates with companies such as Amazon, AT&T, BMW, Facebook, and Google to create its content.

Udacity seems to have found a niche in helping recent college graduates to obtain additional skills to make them more employable. For example, it offers a nanodegree program in digital marketing. This specific program runs for three months and costs $799. If you're cost conscious, you'll be glad to know that the program is offered on a self-directed basis for about half the price.

General Assembly

General Assembly (www.generalassemb.ly) offers short courses, some for free, and full 10- to 12-week courses that you can take on a part-time basis. The company also offers one-week full-time intense versions of these programs. It even has physical campuses throughout the world so you can go in and take some of these courses in a real classroom setting if you prefer.

Like Udacity, General Assembly collaborates with companies on some content, and offers courses on what it calls "today's most in-demand skills." Areas of study include digital marketing, iOS and Android development, data science, data analytics, and product management.

A number of programs offer both online and on-campus versions. The iOS Development Immersive program, for example, is a 12-week full-time program offered in San Francisco. You build iOS apps and become an iOS developer when you're done with the program. The course costs $13,500.

The product management course, on the other hand, runs for ten weeks and is part-time and online. You can also take a full-time accelerated version of this course on campus. The cost is $3,950.

Galvanize

Galvanize (www.galvanize.com) describes itself as the learning community for technology and operates eight campuses in cities throughout the United States. It offers a full-time course in data science that lasts 12 weeks and costs $16,000. It also offers a full-time program in web development that goes for 24 weeks, at a cost of $21,000.

Galvanize also offers a 12-month master's of science degree in data science.

Although not cheap, Galvanize touts a 91 percent placement rate on its site. It helps that the courses offered are in technical areas that are in high demand.

Skillshare

Skillshare (www.skillshare.com) is a learning community focused more on business and the creative arts. The site features more than 17,000 classes, which you can access through a subscription starting at $15 per month or $99 per year. Courses are taught by practitioners in the field, and you can see how users rate them. Most of the classes focus on completing a project.

This resource is great if you want to brush up on your business skills. For example, you can learn about social media marketing and find out how to create email marketing campaigns.

Community College

Last but not least, your local community college is a valuable learning resource that is often overlooked. Most for-profit learning companies offer courses in technical fields and other high-demand and high-paying areas where they can justify charging tuition.

Because community colleges are government funded, they fill an important void by offering classes in fields that may be in demand, but may not pay as much. Examples of these areas include child development and paralegal studies.

If you're looking to supplement your studies with something specific that will help you get a job, or if you know of a course that will help you work more efficiently, be sure to look at your local community college. Tuition tends to be low if not free in some cases. Don't let the price mislead you. Community colleges often have seasoned instructors who come from industry and have relevant expertise.

TIP

The American Association of Community Colleges offers an interactive tool where you can locate your nearest community college. Check it out at `www.aacc.nche.edu/pages/ccfinder.aspx`.

Chapter **18**

Ten (Or So) Potential Benefits Besides Salary

Your salary is only a part of your compensation. Many employers offer other ways for you to earn money or to save it. You can also avoid paying taxes on these savings, increasing the money you set aside. This is because when you save money to a pre-tax account, you aren't paying taxes on that amount of money; instead, you're using that money you would have paid in taxes for medical, commuter, or childcare expenses. Or you can save it for retirement.

Knowing about these perks will help you get a better grasp of your compensation package and your full earning potential. In this chapter, I offer details about some of the most commonly offered benefits.

401(k), 403(b), and 457

These employer-sponsored plans allow you to save for retirement by setting aside "pre-tax" dollars from your paycheck. This is a big advantage because these savings are not taxed as you store them away. Only when you retire do these funds get taxed — but not before many years have passed, and the power of compounding interest has made your savings grow.

Another advantage of having one of these retirement plans is that your employer may provide matching funds, up to a certain percentage of your salary. The types of matching include the following:

>> **Discretionary match:** The employer is not obliged to do this but can match the funds you contribute to your plan at its own discretion. This is usually based on the organization meeting certain revenue, profit, or cash milestones.

>> **Safe harbor match:** In this type of matching, the employer may be required to provide matching in a given year if certain tests are triggered. Specifically, if the organization has a lot of highly compensated employees (HCEs) contributing to their plans and not enough non-HCEs, the employer may need to match the contributions of non-HCEs. These matching contributions are typically 100 percent vested (more on vesting later in this chapter).

>> **Guaranteed match:** In this type of matching, the employer guarantees a match up to a certain percent of your gross salary every year. For example, an employer may match 100 percent of your contribution up to 5 percent of your gross salary. So, if you make $60,000 a year and contribute 4 percent of your gross pay ($2,400 a year) to your 401(k), your employer will put in another $2,400. The percentages will vary by employer, but the idea is that they guarantee a match up to a certain percentage.

TIP

If an employer provides matching, you should take this match into consideration as you evaluate a job offer. You typically become eligible for retirement benefits upon hire or three to six months after your start date; ask your prospective employer when you'll be eligible.

The 401(k) plan is for companies and for-profit businesses. The 403(b) is for public education organizations and nonprofits. Governmental and certain nongovernmental employers offer the 457 plan. Unlike a 401(k), the 457 plan can have independent contractors as participants. Another difference in the 457 plan is that, unlike with a 401(k), there is no penalty for withdrawing money before age 55.

TECHNICAL
STUFF

Your 401(k) may involved something called *vesting*. A stock or option is considered *vested* when you have full right to it. If it's not vested, then it means you don't have a right to it yet. Vesting periods can range from two to five years, depending on the employer and the type of grant you're being given. For example, in the case of certain 401(k) matches made by your employer, you may get a match outright, but if you leave the organization within a two-year period, the employer may have a right to take back its match. In this example, the employer contribution to your 401(k) is said to have a two-year vesting period.

Health Insurance

Health insurance can be expensive, costing hundreds of dollars a month for an individual or even thousands a month for a family. Employers tend to offer health insurance, along with vision and dental insurance, at a reduced monthly cost, referred to as a *premium*. Some employers may cover the entire premium for you; others will make you pay a small part of it.

Just as important as the monthly premium is your *annual deductible*, the amount you pay out of pocket each year before the insurance starts covering your medical expenses. If your deductible is zero, then your insurance starts covering expenses as soon as you're insured. If you have a high deductible, such as $5,000 a year, then you need to pay for the first $5,000 of medical expenses before your insurance starts covering medical costs.

Flexible Spending Accounts, Health Savings Accounts, and Commuter Spending Accounts

Flexible spending accounts (FSAs) are similar to retirement accounts in that they allow you to set aside money before tax. But in this case, the money can be spent on qualified medical expenses such as prescription medicine and dependent-care expenses such as childcare. The advantage of these accounts is that the money you set aside is *never* taxed — not when you set it aside and not even when you spend it. The higher your tax rate, the more you save. For example, if you're in a high tax bracket and pay 30 percent in taxes, $1,000 in income ends up being $700 after taxes, costing you $300 in tax. But if you save $1,000 in a pre-tax account, you get to keep that $300 and use it for medical-related expenses.

Types of savings accounts include the following:

>> **Health FSAs:** These are the most common and allow you to save pre-tax funds for medical expenses such as prescriptions, co-payments for doctor and dentist visits, and birth control. The annual limit of what you can contribute to your individual health FSA is $2,650. If you don't use all your funds for the current year, you can carry forward up to $500 to the following one. The employer keeps any unused amount over this.

TIP

When choosing how much to set aside for your health FSA, do your best to estimate how much you may spend on medical expenses in the coming year so that you have enough money to cover these, but at the same, you don't end up leaving unused money. You can spend the money even before you've contributed it to your account.

>> **Health savings accounts (HSAs):** HSAs are similar to health FSAs. They also allow you to take pre-tax money out of your paycheck for medical expenses. But unlike health FSAs, you don't lose the funds if you don't use them. The money carries over and accumulates, and it's always available to you. HSAs are available to employees who are enrolled in high-deductible health plans, and you can have either an HSA or a health FSA, but not both. As with health FSAs, you can spend the money even before you've contributed it to your account.

In 2018, you can contribute up to $3,450 into a personal HSA account or $6,900 into a family HSA. These limits change periodically, so be sure to check with the IRS at www.irs.gov for the latest information.

>> **Dependent care FSA:** These accounts cover expenses for childcare if you have children under 13 years of age. They also cover elderly care if you have a senior citizen as a dependent. The annual household limit of what you can contribute is $5,000.

Unlike FSA and HSA accounts, with dependent care FSAs, you can only spend what you have contributed so far in a given year.

>> **Commuter spending accounts:** These accounts allow you to save up to $260 per month for parking at work and up to $260 per month for transit expenses to and from work. These accounts are also funded through pre-tax dollars.

REMEMBER

Save your receipts and ask for detailed receipts whenever possible. These accounts often require proof of your purchases before you get reimbursed. For medical visits, the receipt should include your name, the date when the service was provided, and details of the service you received.

Bonus Plans

Bonus plans vary from employer to employer and even within an organization. These plans tie bonus compensation to your individual performance, or your team's goals or to the organization achieving certain milestones. You may be able to participate in one or more of these types of bonus plans at the same time.

Bonuses may consist of cash, stock, or other incentives such as paid travel expenses and educational opportunities.

The frequency of these plans also varies. You can have quarterly bonuses tied to a quarterly goal. Team performance may also be measured quarterly. Bonuses tied to an organization reaching certain goals, such as revenue or profit markers, tend to get paid quarterly or on an annual basis.

Profit-Sharing Plans and Profit-Sharing Retirement Plans

Employers can set up profit-sharing plans at their own discretion. Usually these plans allow employees to earn bonuses based on annual or quarterly profits. These profits are also commonly referred to as *earnings* and are calculated on the organization's after-tax net income. If the company does not make a profit, then the employer does not have to give a bonus.

Profit-sharing retirement plans are similar to profit-sharing plans, but the employer makes a discretionary contribution, based on profits to an employee's retirement account, such as a 401(k). In essence, the employer makes a discretionary contribution to your 401(k), but the match is based on the organization's earnings.

Restricted Stock Units

Restricted stock units (RSUs) are a way for *publicly listed companies* (companies that trade on public stock exchanges such as NASDAQ or the NYSE) or venture capital–backed companies to give stock to employees. These stock units are called *restricted* because they usually vest over a period of time before you get them. They may have other restrictions as well.

RSUs are intended to give you ownership in the company and to provide you with an incentive to grow the value of your shares, and the company, through your hard work. Instead of getting RSUs outright when you start employment, they vest over a number of years. This is to encourage you to stay at the organization until your RSUs vest.

After they vest, these RSUs are considered income and are taxed at your income level. The employer may withhold some of these RSUs in order to cover your tax liability. For example, if your RSUs end up being worth $10,000 and you owe $2,000 in taxes, your employer may keep $2,000 worth of RSUs to cover your tax liability and give you $8,000 in RSUs.

TIP

At some point, you'll most likely leave your first job to pursue another opportunity. Take into account any vesting schedule for RSUs, retirement account matches, or stock options you have, and plan your departure date accordingly so you don't leave money on the table.

Stock Option Plans

Stock options are similar to RSUs in that they're also meant to provide you with an incentive to stay at the company and to help grow its value.

Stock options are not stock. Instead, as the name implies, they're an "option" to buy a certain number of shares at a specified low price. This price is often referred to as the *exercise price* or *strike price.* If you get a chance to sell your shares because the company goes public or gets bought, you make money on the difference between the share price and the exercise price at the time you sell your shares.

WARNING

With opportunity often comes risk. You could encounter a scenario where the company's shares have a certain price, you exercise your options at a lower price, and you decide to keep your shares and not sell them for the moment. This may create a taxable event for you. Then the company's share price may drop sharply, causing you to lose money. On top of that, you may have to pay taxes and not have the money to cover those taxes. Check with a professional tax accountant if you ever find yourself in such a situation.

For example, if you have 1,000 options at an exercise price of $1 per share and the company ends up going public at a price of $10 per share, you make $9 per share. Your total gain is $9,000 because you have 1,000 options.

Options tend to get taxed at the time of exercise.

There are two types of stock options: *incentive stock options* (ISOs), which are available only to employees, and *non-qualified stock options* (NSOs), which can be granted to anyone, including employees, contractors, and advisors. The tax treatment varies for these types of options.

TIP

Check with an accountant about your particular tax circumstances and how ISOs and NSOs affect you. You can also learn more about taxes from the IRS at www.irs.gov.

Tuition Reimbursement

This benefit means what it sounds like. Some employers offer financial assistance to employees who take courses or who are working toward a degree. The amount reimbursed varies by employer, and sometimes the employer requires you to be employed with it for a certain period of time before this benefit kicks in.

Employers may impose certain conditions for tuition reimbursement. You may be required to maintain a certain grade level. The course material should also apply to your work at hand, and often, your studies should contribute toward an advanced degree or certificate.

Employers tend to offer this benefit as a way to attract talent and to grow the capabilities of their workforce.

Index

D

E

About the Author

Roberto Angulo is co-founder and CEO of AfterCollege, the largest career network for college students and recent graduates. He came up with the idea for AfterCollege while studying economics at Stanford University. Not knowing what to do with his degree, he set out to start a service that helped students figure out what to do based on their field of study. Today, AfterCollege is used by millions of students and grads annually and counts more than 18,000 professors and academic contacts as subscribers who receive targeted job content for their students.

Roberto is also the CEO of Recruitology, a leading recruitment platform that helps small and medium employers hire the right candidates at the right time. The platform gives employers access to best-of-breed job sites and includes intelligent job distribution, an applicant tracking system, and analytics.

He collaborated with President Obama's administration on various initiatives, including the launch of Summer Jobs+, which created summer opportunities for youth ages 16 to 24. He also co-founded US2020.org, an initiative to engage STEM professionals as mentors to students from kindergarten through graduate school.

Roberto enjoys traveling, running, and developing new product and partnership ideas for AfterCollege and Recruitology.

Dedication

To the entire team at AfterCollege. Without you, this work would not have been possible. To my wife, Ana Bertran who's been my biggest fan and supporter. She encouraged me to write this book. And to Sophie and Lucas, who think it's really cool that their dad wrote a book.

Author's Acknowledgments

I am extremely grateful to the AfterCollege team, past and present. This work is distilled from years of knowledge gathered and created by the team in the pursuit of our goal to help new job seekers figure out their career path.

To Erik Brynjolfsson, who encouraged me to start AfterCollege, and to the founding team, Ana Bertran, Marc Dee, Brian Heifferon, and Karen Heifferon. To early supporters who believed there was a better way to help new grads find work and who were key in helping get AfterCollege off the ground: Herman DeKesel, Bruce Skillings, Mario Rosati, Ira Dorf, Susan Hailey, Dan Jansen, Vicky Leonard, Giselle Phan, Steve Katelman, and Curtis Rogers. And to later supporters Marcel Legrand, Trevor Loy, Beto Pallares, and Larry Penley.

To Michael Dawes, Steve Girolami, Roxie Crowley, Tim Weaver, Matt Baum and Steph Peterson. Your hard work and dedication has propelled AfterCollege forward.

Also to Chelsea Claure, Carrie McCullagh, Devin Kaylor, Truman Guan, Saan Saeteurn, Perry Lee, Alejandra Salazar, Mike Imperial, Gerard Barcelon, and Pano Santos.

Finally, to the team that leads the day-to-day operations of AfterCollege to help students find their first job: Elizabeth Rodriguez, Javier Suazo, Elena Romanyuk, and Skye Kraft.

Publisher's Acknowledgments

Acquisitions Editor: Amy Fandrei

Project Editor: Elizabeth Kuball

Copy Editor: Elizabeth Kuball

Technical Editor: Jennifer Rutt

Production Editor: Siddique Shaik

Cover Photos: © ConstantinosZ/Shutterstock

Take dummies with you everywhere you go!

Whether you are excited about e-books, want more from the web, must have your mobile apps, or are swept up in social media, dummies makes everything easier.

Find us online!

dummies
A Wiley Brand

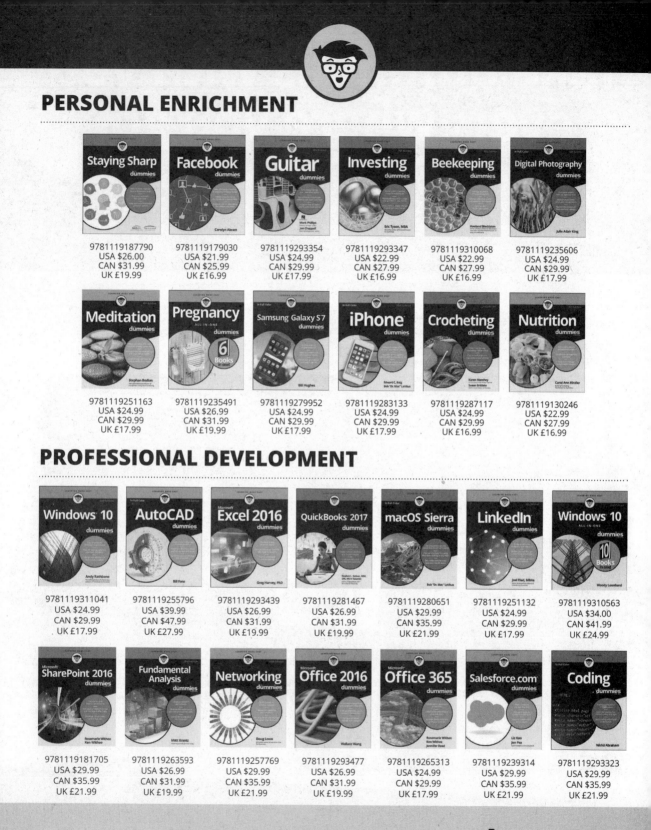

PERSONAL ENRICHMENT

Staying Sharp
9781119187790
USA $26.00
CAN $31.99
UK £19.99

Facebook
9781119179030
USA $21.99
CAN $25.99
UK £16.99

Guitar
9781119293354
USA $24.99
CAN $29.99
UK £17.99

Investing
9781119293347
USA $22.99
CAN $27.99
UK £16.99

Beekeeping
9781119310068
USA $22.99
CAN $27.99
UK £16.99

Digital Photography
9781119235606
USA $24.99
CAN $29.99
UK £17.99

Meditation
9781119251163
USA $24.99
CAN $29.99
UK £17.99

Pregnancy
9781119235491
USA $26.99
CAN $31.99
UK £19.99

Samsung Galaxy S7
9781119279952
USA $24.99
CAN $29.99
UK £17.99

iPhone
9781119283133
USA $24.99
CAN $29.99
UK £17.99

Crocheting
9781119287117
USA $24.99
CAN $29.99
UK £16.99

Nutrition
9781119130246
USA $22.99
CAN $27.99
UK £16.99

PROFESSIONAL DEVELOPMENT

Windows 10
9781119311041
USA $24.99
CAN $29.99
UK £17.99

AutoCAD
9781119255796
USA $39.99
CAN $47.99
UK £27.99

Excel 2016
9781119293439
USA $26.99
CAN $31.99
UK £19.99

QuickBooks 2017
9781119281467
USA $26.99
CAN $31.99
UK £19.99

macOS Sierra
9781119280651
USA $29.99
CAN $35.99
UK £21.99

LinkedIn
9781119251132
USA $24.99
CAN $29.99
UK £17.99

Windows 10
9781119310563
USA $34.00
CAN $41.99
UK £24.99

SharePoint 2016
9781119181705
USA $29.99
CAN $35.99
UK £21.99

Fundamental Analysis
9781119263593
USA $26.99
CAN $31.99
UK £19.99

Networking
9781119257769
USA $29.99
CAN $35.99
UK £21.99

Office 2016
9781119293477
USA $26.99
CAN $31.99
UK £19.99

Office 365
9781119265313
USA $24.99
CAN $29.99
UK £17.99

Salesforce.com
9781119239314
USA $29.99
CAN $35.99
UK £21.99

Coding
9781119293323
USA $29.99
CAN $35.99
UK £21.99